"We all have an enormous sphere of influence, though we're not always aware of the influence we have. After you read *The Difference You Make*, you'll never take your influence for granted again. Pat Williams gives you all the tools you need to refine, enrich, and expand your influence on the world around you."

—**Mike Smith**, Atlanta Falcons head coach

"As coaches, we are challenged on a daily basis to give the young people we work with the tools to be successful in life. We hope to show them what it means to think of others before themselves, to never set limits to their goals and dreams, and to always reach for the pinnacle of achievement. Sometimes we as teachers can use a road map of our own, a means of encouragement to remind us what we can do in our position to help shape the next generation. Pat has made this one of his important and guiding principles, and in this book, he shows just how we can use our influence for a positive purpose. This should be recommended reading, not only for coaches, but for people in all walks of life, as a blueprint of what is possible in our role as difference-makers."

—**Muffet McGraw**, University of Notre Dame head women's basketball coach

"Pat Williams has spent the majority of his life influencing people to help make them better. His guidance for all of those he has touched has helped shape many successful lives. I know of no one more capable of helping others realize their potential and the 'difference they can make' more than Pat Williams."

—**Terry Collins**, New York Mets manager

"Pat Williams is a man of great influence in his book *The Difference You Make*. I love the way he reminds us that we all have the power to influence and be influenced. Pat challenges us and encourages us to accept that role to become a positive difference in the lives of others."

—**Leslie Frazier**, Minnesota Vikings head coach

"As a longtime coach in the NFL, I have always believed in the power of influence. After all, if you're not influencing others in a positive way, then what are you living for? In *The Difference You Make*, Pat Williams not only inspires us to be people of influence, but he gives us the practical steps and tools we need to impact others in a powerful way."

—**Romeo Crennel**, Kansas City Chiefs head coach

"I've read Pat Williams's *The Difference You Make*, and I really enjoyed it. This book is packed with valuable new insights about how to have a powerful, positive impact on people in your life. Read it and put these principles into practice. This book is a game changer."

—**Don Mattingly**, Los Angeles Dodgers manager

"Pat Williams always does an outstanding job in each of his books in terms of sharing life lessons through his personal stories. *The Difference*

You Make resonated with me because the focus is the impact and influence you can have on others, and how that defines you as a person more than anything. That's why I enjoy coaching and why I think coaching is one of the greatest professions—you have the ability to impact the lives of young people each and every day. Pat has certainly impacted many people in a positive way through his life, and this book shares some great stories of how Pat and others attained success because of the influence other people had with them along the way."

—**Nick Saban**, University of Alabama head football coach

"As we move forward in life we realize that motivation from others is so short lived. The people who truly inspire us and influence us stand out in our lives and stand the test of time. Pat Williams has captured those people and qualities so well in this latest work of art, *The Difference You Make*. Using this book will be a force."

—**Tom Crean**, Indiana University head men's basketball coach

"I've known Pat Williams for over fifty years and can assure you that he understands the impact of influence we have on others. Stop what you're doing and start reading Pat's latest book. It'll be a life-changer for you!"

—**Jon McGlocklin**, Milwaukee Bucks
longtime player and broadcaster

"If you want to live a life of significance, then live to impact others! *The Difference You Make* is an indispensable resource for all people of influence. In its pages, Pat Williams gives you the practical insights and powerful motivation you need to live a life of influence in your home, your workplace, your community, and your world."

—**Dr. Tony Evans**, The Urban Alternative founder and president

"Pat Williams didn't just write the book on influence. He's lived a life of influence as a father to nineteen kids, as a sports executive, and as an author and speaker. In *The Difference You Make*, Pat shows you, step by step, how to have a powerful, positive, lasting impact on the world by influencing the people around you—one person at a time."

—**Dabo Swinney**, Clemson University Tigers head football coach

"I have read every book by Pat Williams, and *The Difference You Make* is one of my favorites. Upon reading this book, every reader will come to realize that each of us has the ability to make a difference."

—**Steve Alford**, University of New Mexico head basketball coach

"Pat Williams has written a crucial book for these troubled times. Now, more than ever, we need people of influence who will step up and challenge the status quo. *The Difference You Make* will give you the inspiration, motivation, and practical tools to make a positive impact on your world and on generations to come."

—**John Calipari**, University of Kentucky head men's
basketball coach, 2012 NCAA Basketball Champions

THE
Difference
YOU
MAKE

THE

YOU
MAKE

Changing Your World through
the Impact of Your Influence

PAT WILLIAMS
with JIM DENNEY

Revell

a division of Baker Publishing Group
Grand Rapids, Michigan

Published by Revell
a division of Baker Publishing Group
P.O. Box 6287, Grand Rapids, MI 49516-6287
www.revellbooks.com

Printed in the United States of America

Library of Congress Cataloging-in-Publication Data
Williams, Pat.
    The difference you make : changing your world through the impact of your influence / Pat Williams with Jim Denney.
        p.   cm.
    Includes bibliographical references.
    ISBN 978-0-8007-2168-8 (hardcover : alk. paper)
    1. Influence (Psychology) 2. Leadership. 3. Persuasion (Psychology)
    4. Influence (Psychology)—Religious aspects—Christianity. I. Denney, Jim, 1953– II. Title
    BF774.W55 2013
    158.2—dc23   2012034359

Unless otherwise indicated, Scripture taken from the HOLY BIBLE, NEW INTERNA-TIONAL VERSION®. Copyright © 1973, 1978, 1984 Biblica. Used by permission of Zondervan. All rights reserved.

Scripture quotations identified THE MESSAGE are from *The Message* by Eugene H. Peterson, copyright © 1993, 1994, 1995, 2000, 2001, 2002. Used by permission of NavPress Publishing Group. All rights reserved.

Scripture quotations identified PHILLIPS are from The New Testament in Modern English, revised edition—J. B. Phillips, translator. © J. B. Phillips 1958, 1960, 1972. Used by permission of Macmillan Publishing Co., Inc.

Scripture quotations identified KJV are from the King James Version of the Bible.

13   14   15   16   17   18   19   7   6   5   4   3   2   1

I dedicate this book
to three of my grandsons,
Austin, Anthony, and Max.

May they grow up to truly understand
the impact of their influence.

Contents

Foreword

*L*ife is all about influence.

I remind myself every day that God didn't give me the privilege of being a baseball player and manager all these years just for my own enjoyment. He gave me a position of influence, and He expects me to use it wisely.

Recently, before a Yankees-Phillies spring training game in Clearwater, Florida, I saw a man in the stands wearing a CC Sabathia jersey, holding up a hand-lettered sign that read, "Please Remember Steven E. Smith." I recognized the man as Matt Smith, father of Yankees super-fan Steven Smith who had died in a car accident. Steven was just twenty-four years old, and had been hoping for a career in sports broadcasting.

As a father, my heart went out to Matt Smith. I could only imagine what he had gone through in the year and a half since his son died. So I went over and talked to him for a few moments, and we chatted about Steven and what a great young man he was. I invited Matt to meet some of the players, and I arranged to have his poster signed by the whole team.

It didn't take much time or effort on my part to chat with Matt Smith. But I wanted Matt to know that the Yankees remembered Steven and were all touched by his love for the team. I wanted to do anything I could to lift Matt's spirits and lessen his grief, even a little. That was one way all of us on the team could use our influence to help another human being.

Leadership is about influence. During my playing days, I wore number 25 on my jersey. When I took the job as manager of the New York Yankees, I wore number 27. Why? Influence. The Yankees had won twenty-six World Series titles, and I wanted to wear a visible reminder of our goal, a twenty-seventh championship.

Two years after I took the job, we reached that goal. So now, of course, I wear number 28. It's about motivation. It's about focus. It's about keeping the vision always before our eyes as a team. And it's about influence.

After we won the World Series in 2009, we had a great celebration at Yankee Stadium. Late that night, I was driving home along the Cross County Parkway. Approaching a curve in the parkway, I saw a car that had crashed into a wall and was disabled in the opposing lanes. It was a blind curve, and I knew that other drivers, going eighty miles an hour at night, might not be able to avoid the crashed car. So I pulled over, called 911, and went to help the driver of the car. Fortunately, she was not badly hurt.

Situations pop up when we least expect them, and we have to be ready to respond and help each other at a moment's notice. I believe God put me on that road at that moment so that I could have a positive influence on the situation.

The more we are able to see our lives, our careers, our families, and the crises that come our way as opportunities for influence, the more God can use us to make a difference in the lives of others. That's why I'm glad Pat Williams has written this much-needed book, *The Difference You Make: Changing Your World through the Impact of Your Influence.*

This book is packed with stories and insights that are guaranteed to impact your life in a big way. Pat opens up his own life and talks revealingly about his battle with multiple myeloma, his experiences as one of the top executives in professional sports, and his amazing journey as a father of nineteen children, including fourteen by international adoption. And he also tells many stories about other people who have influenced his life or have influenced the world. These stories are riveting and they reveal to us how we can become more effective influencers of the people around us.

These pages are your quick-start guide to becoming a more influential mentor, parent, and leader. You'll gain practical insights into how to become a more positive influence through your words and your actions. And you'll learn how to acquire the character traits and people skills that will enable you to impact the next generation, the people around you, and your society.

Everyone has influence, no matter what your personality type or your career, no matter whether you are rich or poor, married or single, young or old. The question is not whether or not you have influence, but what you will do with the influence you have.

Use your influence wisely. Let Pat Williams show you how. God bless you on your journey.

Joe Girardi, manager, New York Yankees

Acknowledgments

With deep appreciation I acknowledge the support and guidance of the following people who helped make this book possible:

Special thanks to Dan DeVos, Alex Martins, and Rich DeVos of the Orlando Magic.

Hats off to my associate, Andrew Herdliska; my proofreader, Ken Hussar; and my ace typist, Fran Thomas.

Thanks also to my writing partner, Jim Denney, for his superb contributions in shaping this manuscript.

Hearty thanks also go to Andrea Doering, senior acquisition editor at Revell Books, and to the entire Revell team for their vision and insight, and for believing that we had something important to say in these pages.

And, finally, special thanks and appreciation go to my wife, Ruth, and to my wonderful and supportive family. They are truly the backbone of my life.

Introduction

Influence is a funny thing. It's hard to define. It's even hard to describe it. But you know when someone has it. You know when somebody doesn't. No doubt you're aware of the people who influence you. But you may not be sure why they have so much leverage in your life.

Andy Stanley, *Visioneering*[1]

I went in for a routine physical on January 7, 2011—an all-day Orlando Magic executive physical, lasting from 7:00 a.m. to 5:00 p.m. It was one of those intensive workups you'd get at the Cooper Clinic in Dallas or the Mayo Clinic in Rochester, Minnesota. At the end of the day, Dr. Christine Edwards told me, "Well, everything looks good—except there's something in your blood work that doesn't look quite right. At your convenience, you ought to get that checked."

Except for that one small caveat, it was a clean bill of health. Two days later, I ran the Disney Marathon—the fifty-eighth marathon of my career. I felt good all the way to the finish line.

Three days later, I woke up with an explosion of horrible pain in my back. I had never felt pain like that before, even after a marathon. I knew something was terribly wrong—maybe a slipped disk, a pulled muscle, or a nerve problem. I made an appointment with a back specialist. They did a series of x-rays and an MRI, and word came back that everything was fine—they found nothing wrong with my back.

So I went to my primary care physician, Dr. Vince Wilson, who by that time had caught up with the blood work Dr. Edwards had performed. He sat me down in his office with a very troubled look on his face. He shook his head and said, "Why do bad things happen to all the good people?"

I said, "What do you mean, Doc?"

"There's something wrong with your blood work, Pat. There's an abnormal level of protein in your blood. I have a suspicion as to what this means. I hope I'm wrong, but I'm sending you over to see Dr. Robert B. Reynolds, who's a leading expert in this field."

That was on Thursday, January 13, and Dr. Wilson told me my appointment with Dr. Reynolds was for the following Monday, the seventeenth. I had no clue what was going on—and to tell you the truth, I didn't really want a clue. But over the weekend, I began steeling myself for some troubling news.

On Monday, I went to see Dr. Reynolds, and I wasn't even sure what his area of specialization was. It turned out that he was an oncologist and hematologist. Dr. Reynolds told me, "It looks like multiple myeloma—a cancer of the blood and bone marrow." Hearing that, my blood and bone marrow turned to Jell-O.

"We're going to do a couple of tests right away," Dr. Reynolds continued, "and I'll get back to you next week to tell you exactly what we're dealing with." The tests involved a full-body x-ray of my skeleton and an extraction of bone marrow from my hip.

The following week, I went back to Dr. Reynolds' office, accompanied by my wife, Ruth. Dr. Reynolds told us, "It's definite. You have multiple myeloma."

"How curable is it?"

"I'm afraid it's not curable, Pat. But it is very treatable. The goal is remission. With chemotherapy, I'd say you've got about a 70 to 75 percent chance of remission. And by the way, you'd much rather have multiple myeloma today than twenty years ago. That's how far we've come."

At that point, I had an inspiration. "How about this for a motivational slogan: 'The Mission Is Remission.'"

"That's it exactly! You've got many factors in your favor, Pat. Your positive attitude is very important. Your good fitness level is another factor—I don't get to treat many marathoners. Your strong faith is another fact. And, of course, there's the love of your family and the support of the Magic organization."

"Well, what do we do now?"

"We go after it with all we've got. We start chemo, we start oral medication, we get after this as hard as we can. And quickly."

"Okay, Dr. Reynolds," I said. "I'm in your hands. I'll be an obedient patient."

Impacted by Influence

There were two major issues I had to address as I began treatment. First, how do I tell my nineteen children? As the father of four birth children, fourteen children by adoption, and one by remarriage, all of whom are grown and moved away, it was a formidable task—both logistically and emotionally—to contact each one and explain this diagnosis. But we got to all of them—and their reactions to the news were as individual as could be. Some were calm. Some were distraught. Some were emotional. Others were stoic. But all were supportive and pledged to pray for me.

The second major issue: How should I release the information to the public? I met with the Orlando Magic staff and explained the situation, and they helped me come up with a plan for presenting it publicly. The Magic's media director, Joel Glass, scheduled a press conference in February.

Dr. Reynolds sat beside me at the press conference. Ruth and several of our grown children stood behind me as we made the announcement. Dr. Reynolds took the roomful of reporters to med school and explained what multiple myeloma is and how we were going to treat it.

At the end of the press conference, I removed my jacket to reveal the T-shirt underneath. Lettered across the front of it was my new slogan, THE MISSION IS REMISSION—and it was greeted with cheers and applause.

The reporters carried the message to the greater public. I was totally unprepared for what happened next.

Over the days and weeks that followed, I was overwhelmed with emails, cards, letters, and phone calls. I received best wishes from people I had known from my school days, college days, minor league baseball days, and throughout my NBA career. Many of them told me of something I had done or said that had impacted their lives in some way. More often than not, my reaction was, "Wow, I don't remember doing that. I don't remember saying that."

Throughout all of those years, without even realizing it, I had been impacting and influencing other lives. I was amazed to discover that, in many cases, it was a *lasting* influence. I might have forgotten some act I did, a phone call I made, a card I sent, a word of encouragement I offered—but other people remembered. What *I* remember is not important. What *they* remember is what I call "the impact of influence."

I also received calls and emails from people I had never met, but who had heard me speak or had read my books. All of those hundreds of communications were touching and life-affirming, and I read each one. It was as if I had died and had the privilege of hearing my own eulogy—a thousand times over. That experience prompted me to reflect on the impact we all have on others around us—even when we are completely unaware of our influence.

Then I thought of all the people who had impacted my own life during my boyhood, adolescence, and young adulthood. I thought of my teachers and coaches at Tower Hill School in Wilmington, Delaware, my instructors and coaches at Wake

Forest University, my employers during my minor league baseball career and throughout my NBA career.

As a boy, I hung around ballparks and stadiums, collecting autographs. Through my friendship with Ruly Carpenter, son of Philadelphia Phillies owner Bob Carpenter, I got to go down to spring training and rub shoulders with major league ballplayers. To this day, I can tell you chapter and verse on every one of them—and what a thrill it was to hear some of my heroes recognize me and call me by name! All of those influences on my life are still right here, etched in my soul.

So I have been deeply influenced by people of greatness throughout my life—and in my own way, I've tried to have a positive impact on the people within my own sphere of influence. Since my diagnosis, all of the calls, cards, and letters I've received have helped to trigger and shape the book you are reading right now. In many ways, the diagnosis of multiple myeloma has turned out to be a blessing—and an opportunity.

I believe this illness came about in God's own timing. I was diagnosed at about the same time as the release of my book *Coach Wooden: The Seven Principles That Shaped His Life and Will Change Yours*. As it went out into the marketplace I was flooded with messages from people touched by the book's message. Many of the notes went something like this: "Even though I never met Coach Wooden, your book makes me want to be like him. Coach has influenced me greatly, just through the pages of this book. And so have you."

We all have influence, we all have an impact on the people around us—and we have all been shaped and impacted by the influencers in our own lives. The goal of this book is to help you to become more intentional and strategic in the use of your influence. Throughout these pages, I'll talk about the people who have shaped my life, and the various ways I've tried to influence the lives of others in a positive way—as a father, teacher, mentor, businessman, spokesman, public speaker, author, leader, and Christian. I'll tell stories of influential people from all walks of life.

As you read, I hope you'll find insights that will inspire you to thoughtfully, intentionally impact the lives of others with your influence. I hope you'll use this book as your road map to a lifetime of deeper, wider, more profound influence. Use the discussion questions after each chapter for either personal reflection or group discussion. Take out your highlighter or your pen and make notes in the margin. If you have ideas or questions, go to the contact page at the end of the book and get in touch with me.

Think of this book as a two-way chat between friends. I'm eager to see how this book will impact you, and how you will turn around and impact my life. So thanks for opening this book and reading this far. I'm happy to meet you, and glad to discover another person who shares my passion for influencing others.

Let's talk.

1

The Influences
That Have Shaped Your Life

I'm no self-made man. . . . I am who I am because of
those who cared enough about me to touch my soul.

Mark Tabb, *Living with Less*[1]

graduated from Wake Forest University in the spring of 1962,
played minor league baseball with the Miami Marlins during
the summer, then attended Indiana University in Bloomington in the fall, pursuing a master's in physical education. While
in Bloomington, I met Mom Burgher.

Her name was Mid, but everybody called her "Mom," though
she had no children of her own. Mom and her husband Bob
ran Burgher's Grill on Main Street in Bloomington. It was an
eatery straight out of a Norman Rockwell painting. Everybody
in Bloomington ate there, from the chamber of commerce big-
wigs to the students from the university.

The food was great, but that's not what drew people to
Burgher's Grill. People came to talk to Mom. She was a great

listener, and she knew how to get anyone talking about their hopes and dreams, their successes and disappointments. Mom was probably the best amateur psychologist and motivator in the world. Whenever you walked out of Burgher's Grill after a talk with Mom, you felt you could take on the world.

Though the Burghers had no children, Mom had hundreds of sons. She called all the athletes and coaches at Indiana University "my boys." I can still picture her at football and baseball games, decked out in Indiana red, cheering her lungs out for her boys. When the team went on the road, she'd show up to see the players board the bus and then greet them when they returned. Win or lose, Mom was always rooting for you.

Mom didn't keep business hours. If a guy was ever homesick, or had girlfriend trouble or problems at school, he could go to the Burghers' house, knock on the door, and find a listening ear. Mom always kept snacks handy, because it's easier to pour out your troubles over a plate of cookies and a glass of milk.

I spent two years in Bloomington, and I was in Mom's home many times. I vividly remember the pictures on the walls—pictures of Mom's boys, the many young men she had influenced over the years. There were photos of young men in football uniforms and army uniforms, photos of young men with wives and little kids, pictures of young men living out the dreams they had shared with Mom over a burger and shake so many years earlier. Mom Burgher had impacted those young men and encouraged them to believe in their dreams.

Even after Bob Burgher passed away, Mom kept right on influencing young lives until she herself passed away in her eighties. She left quite a legacy. For more than half a century, she empowered Indiana athletes—including a skinny twenty-two-year-old kid named Williams, who was far away from home. Mom got to know me well. She knew all about my family and my dreams for the future. She kept track of me and sent me notes and cards long after I left Indiana. And for years afterward, whenever I happened to be anywhere near Bloomington, I'd go out of my way to visit Mom.

I don't know if Mom Burgher ever said to herself, "I want to devote my life to having a positive influence on the lives of young men at Indiana University." I think it came naturally to her. Being an influencer, an encourager, and an empowerer was just who she was. It was her gift. Now more than ever, the world needs people like Mom Burgher—people who are willing to be guides, counselors, mentors, role models, friends, and encouragers.

Wouldn't you like to leave a legacy like Mom Burgher? Maybe the reason you care so much about your own influence is that, somewhere along the line, there was a "Mom Burgher" in your life—a "proxy parent" who was there for you in those times when you were a little uncertain and far from home—a guiding friend who always left the porch light on in case you might stop by.

As I write about some of the people who have made a difference in my life, I pray that some of my experiences will resonate with you. As I tell you about some of the people who have influenced me, I believe some familiar faces will come to your mind, maybe people you haven't thought about in years. As we remember the people who have shaped our lives, we can't help but be inspired and motivated to become people of influence as well.

Major League Lessons from the Minor Leagues

In 1963, after two summers with the minor league Miami Marlins, I faced the fact that it would take more than a .205 batting average to get me to the major leagues. So I reluctantly let go of the baseball dreams I had nurtured since I was seven years old. Instead, I pursued a new dream of front-office sports management.

I've spent half a century as a sports executive, and one of the great influencers who opened that door for me was Bill Durney, the general manager of the Miami Marlins. I got to know Bill during my two years as a player and my third year as a front-office neophyte. I knew I needed a mentor if I was going to succeed in the sports world, so I went to Bill and told him, "I need an education in pro baseball, and you know more about the baseball business than anyone else I've ever known. Would you show me how to run a baseball organization?"

Bill Durney graciously took me under his wing. Over the next few months, I was always at his side, even living in his home for a while. Bill was my mentor and coach. I scooped up every scrap of wisdom and insight he had to offer. He was a great friend and teacher until his death in 1968. I would never have achieved anything in this business without the impact he had on my life.

In February 1965, I moved from Miami to Spartanburg, South Carolina, to take over as general manager of the Spartanburg Phillies. I was twenty-four years old and had orders to report to Mr. R. E. Littlejohn, one of the team owners. He wasn't home when I arrived, but his wife told me, "You'll never meet another man like Mr. R. E." I soon discovered that his wife was right.

Mr. R. E. Littlejohn was one of the wisest men I've ever known, and I was fortunate that he practically adopted me as his own son. My own father had died in 1962, when I was twenty-two. Mr. Littlejohn became my stand-in dad when I was twenty-four, and he remained a guiding figure in my life until his death in 1987. He was simply the most exemplary man I've ever known, and I wanted to be like him. He made such a profound impact on my life that I named my firstborn son James Littlejohn Williams.

I ended up running the Spartanburg Phillies for four years, 1965 to 1968, and Mr. Littlejohn became my mentor, my encourager, and my best friend. He was a key factor in my conversion to faith in Jesus Christ. When I look back on those four years with Mr. Littlejohn, I can see my younger self as he must have seen me: impetuous, impatient, and rough around the edges. My attitude was, "I want everything, and I want it now!" Mr. Littlejohn loved my enthusiasm and drive, but he knew that those qualities needed to be channeled and brought to maturity if I was to reach my full potential. So day by day, Mr. R. E. Littlejohn instructed me and impacted my young life.

Our ballpark in Spartanburg was a "dry" park—we didn't serve beer and we didn't even have wall signs advertising alcoholic beverages. When I took over as general manager, I didn't realize that the lack of beer ads at the ballpark was due to Mr. R. E.'s personal policy. So I went to Mr. Littlejohn and said, "Sir, we could make a lot of money if we sold beer in the park and took in wall ads for beer."

He looked at me as if I had just uttered blasphemy. "Pat!" he said sternly. "If I we did that, I'd have to sell the team!"

Then Mr. R. E. explained to me that he was extremely careful about the impression he made on other people—and especially on the young people of our community. He believed alcoholic beverages had a corrupting influence on the young, so he would not allow any hint of alcohol on the premises.

I learned a lesson that has stuck with me throughout my career: Always be aware of the impact of your influence on others.

In July 1968, I received a phone call from Dr. Jack Ramsay, who was then head coach of the NBA's Philadelphia 76ers. He invited me to become the 76ers' business manager. I told Mr. Littlejohn and his business partner, Leo Hughes, about this offer, and they agreed it was a big career move for me. Though I'd be leaving baseball, I'd be moving into the big leagues of basketball.

Mr. R. E. said, "You're ready to make this move, Pat—but I hate to lose you. If you'd stay here in Spartanburg, Mr. Hughes and I would give you the ball club."

I was stunned. "Give me the ball club? You don't mean you'd—"

"We'd sign everything over to you, lock, stock, and ballpark. You'd be the owner. It's all yours—if you want it. All you have to do is stay."

Mr. Littlejohn was the kindest man I'd ever known—and at that moment I knew he truly loved me like the son he never had. In today's terms, a ball club like the Spartanburg Phillies would be worth well over $6 million—and Mr. Littlejohn was offering it to me as a gift, wrapped up like a Christmas present!

Oh, I was tempted. Many times I've wondered if I should have taken him up on it—but I couldn't shake the feeling that it was time to move on.

So, with Mr. Littlejohn's blessing, I went to Philadelphia and became a front-office executive in the NBA. For the next three decades, as I moved to the Chicago Bulls, then to the Atlanta Hawks, then back to the 76ers, and finally to the founding of the Orlando Magic, I never made a major decision or career move without talking to Mr. Littlejohn.

Once, over a seafood dinner, I told him, "You know, I went to Wake Forest for my BS and Indiana University for my MS, but I got my PhD from Littlejohn University." He laughed and humbly waved off my compliment—but I meant it. I learned more from the influence of Mr. R. E. than from all my years of higher education.

When Mr. R. E. passed away, I felt I had lost a father for the second time. But in a real sense, he hasn't left. Mr. R. E. Little-john lives on in my life and the lives of literally thousands of people he has impacted over the years. To this day, whenever I face a difficult decision, I ask myself, "What would Mr. Little-john do?"—and I have my answer.

Rhymes with "Wreck"

I was twenty-two years old when Bill Durney introduced me to Hall of Fame baseball owner-promoter Bill Veeck. (In case you're wondering, Veeck rhymes with "wreck.") Bill Veeck impacted my life like a 95-mile-an-hour fastball. More than any of my mentors, he taught me the value of *fun*.

The son of a Chicago sportswriter, Bill got into baseball by hawking peanuts, popcorn, and scorecards in the stands at Wrigley Field. He was mentored by Chicago Cubs manager Charley Grimm in the 1930s and '40s, and got into baseball ownership by purchasing struggling teams and transforming them into crowd-pleasers. He took a Cubs farm team, the Milwaukee

Brewers, from last place to first in just three seasons. In 1946, Veeck led an ownership syndicate that bought the broken-down Cleveland Indians—and two years later, the Indians won the World Series. He later owned the St. Louis Browns and the Chicago White Sox.

Bill Veeck was a promotional genius—and a great humanitarian. At a time when racism was institutionalized in American society, Bill looked at people as *people*, and he didn't care what race you were. In 1947, he brought Larry Doby to the Cleveland Indians—the first black player in the American League—and he later brought Satchel Paige up from the Negro League to play for Cleveland.

In his 1962 autobiography, *Veeck—As in Wreck*, he wrote, "My philosophy as a baseball operator could not be more simple. It is to create the greatest enjoyment for the greatest number of people. Not by detracting from the ball game, but by adding a few moments of fairly simple pleasure. My intention was always to draw people to the park and make baseball fans out of them."[2]

After my first year as general manager of the Spartanburg Phillies, I felt like a failure because we'd had a losing season. I was mentally and physically exhausted after working day and night for six months, absolutely draining myself in a failed effort to turn the Phillies around. What had all those sixteen-hour days accomplished? I had an empty feeling, a sense that all my effort had been wasted. It would have been one thing if I had at least failed in the attempt to cure cancer or bring about world peace. But I hadn't even succeeded in my rather modest goal of producing a winning season for the fans in Spartanburg.

So I called Bill Veeck and shared with him my sense of confusion, discouragement, and disillusionment. He listened patiently; then he said, "Pat, how many people did you draw to the ballpark during the season?"

"One hundred fourteen thousand."

"Did they have a good time?" he asked. "Were they entertained? How much fun did they have?"

"They had a lot of fun. Win or lose, people came up to me and told me what a great time they had."

"Well," Bill said, "tell me one other thing you could have done this summer that would have provided as much fun for the good citizens of Spartanburg?"

"I can't think of anything else we could have done."

"Pat," he said, "you never, ever have to apologize for showing people a fun time. If you made people happy, you did your job. You're a success."

With those words, Bill Veeck transformed my thinking. Sure, we'd had a losing season, but we had entertained the fans—and we'd made a profit. Throughout the years that followed, in good times and bad, I could hear Bill's voice in my ear, reminding me that if I was selling *fun*, I was successful.

Bill Veeck was my mentor, my friend, and my role model. He impacted my life by the power of his influence. The lessons he taught me almost five decades ago still shape my life, my attitude, and my decisions to this day.

In July 1969, Bill Veeck called and told me that a friend of his, Phil Frye of Chicago, wanted to talk with me. Phil was one of the eight owners of the struggling Chicago Bulls NBA franchise. I would later discover that Frye had a summer home in Tryon, North Carolina, near Spartanburg, and had come to many of our games. Frye knew all about my crazy promotions as a minor league general manager. He'd seen how I revitalized the Spartanburg Phillies, and thought I could help turn the Bulls around.

When I was in Spartanburg, I had no idea who Phil Frye was. I had greeted him at the gates on numerous occasions, but he'd never introduced himself. Only a couple of years later did I learn that there had been an NBA owner at our games, and that I had left a big impression on him.

The first time I met with Phil Frye, he told me the team was making no money and drawing few fans. This was long before the Michael Jordan era (in fact, Jordan was a first-grader at that time). Even though the Bulls were struggling through hard times, Chicago was a great sports town, and I knew we could put the Bulls on the map.

Phil Frye became my mentor, my sounding board, and my psychiatrist during my challenging years in Chicago. Throughout my four-year stint with the Bulls, Phil insisted I have lunch with him at the Chicago Club once a month. Phil and I just clicked, and he was a great friend during those years.

One of the biggest lessons I had to learn as a general manager was how to work with strong personalities like George Steinbrenner, who had a minority interest in the Bulls. George would call me several times a week, demanding to know about this decision or that individual or some player we had signed or traded. He really wanted to run the team—and every time I picked up the phone and heard his secretary say, "Please hold for Mr. Steinbrenner," I had a Maalox moment. Phil Frye helped me to understand George and not be intimidated by his blustery personality.

Phil was a fount of advice and encouragement. If not for Phil Frye and his willingness to impact my life with his influence, I never would have made it in Chicago. Even when Phil Frye was no longer a Bulls owner, he continued to meet with me, mentor me, and look out for me. I think he felt a sense of responsibility because he had a key role in putting me in that job at such a young age, and he wanted to make sure the job didn't eat me alive.

"I'm the Head Cheerleader!"

You never outgrow the need for the impact of influence in your life. One of the great influencers of my life today is Rich DeVos, the billionaire co-founder of Amway and chairman of RDV Sports, which owns the Orlando Magic. Rich has been one of the key mentors in my personal and professional life for as long as I've known him. I turn to Rich for advice and insight whenever I'm facing a tough problem or decision.

In July 1995, when my first marriage was coming to an end, I knew I had to issue a statement to the media. I spent an entire day writing multiple drafts of a press release. Finally, after hours of labor, I had crafted an eloquent two-page press release. Then I showed it to Rich.

He read it through, then said, "Pat, you don't need to say all that." Then he dictated three simple sentences that captured the heart of what I needed to say. It was some of the best advice I have ever received, and it was one of the many ways Rich DeVos has impacted my life through his wisdom and character.

In the wake of my diagnosis of multiple myeloma, Rich DeVos has impacted my life through his words and his example. At age eighty-six, Rich has faced his own mortality several times, surviving cancer, strokes, multiple bypass surgery, and a heart transplant at age seventy-one. My life has been profoundly affected as I have watched him go through these experiences, and as he has encouraged me through my own health crisis.

Rich lives each day to lift up and encourage other people. If you ask him what his role has been at Amway and the Orlando Magic, he'll say, "I'm the head cheerleader!" And it's true. Rich DeVos has an amazing ability to motivate, inspire, and impact people in a powerful way.

When we talk, it's never a superficial exchange. Rich gets right down to reality and wants to know my joys, hurts, and struggles. He asks, "Is there anything you need? Any way I can support you? Any need in your life I can pray for?" And he always concludes with a word of encouragement: "You're doing a great job. This never would have happened without you." The impact of his influence in my life is amazing.

As I began working on this book, I received an email from a lady in India who asked if I could help her get a message to Rich DeVos. So I passed her request on to Rich. A few days later, I received another note from the lady, saying, "Thanks so much for conveying my message to Rich DeVos. I received a hand-written note from him just now, and it made my day!"

Rich is famous for his handwritten notes; I have three of them framed on my wall. He always signs his notes, "Love Ya! Rich." Whether he knows you personally or not, Rich really does love you, because he loves everybody, encourages everybody, and motivates everybody whose life he touches.

Why does Rich do that? There's no profit in sending out a handwritten note to a lady halfway around the world, a lady he will never meet. There's no profit in sending these notes of encouragement to any of us. But Rich doesn't influence others in order to get something for himself. Instead, he continually *gives of himself* to others. He is committed to living out the impact of influence. He knows that God has blessed his business so that he could have a worldwide platform—and he uses that platform to bless and influence others.

Tom Peters, co-author of *In Search of Excellence*, is a big believer in the power and impact of a simple little handwritten note. He writes:

> We wildly underestimate the power of the tiniest personal touch. And of all personal touches, I find the short, handwritten "nice job" note to have the greatest impact. (It even seems to beat a call—something about the tangibility.)
>
> A former boss (who's gone on to a highly successful career) religiously took about 15 minutes (max) at the end of each day, at 5:30, 6:30, whenever, to jot a half-dozen paragraph-long notes to people who'd given him time during the day, or who'd made a provocative remark at some meeting. I remember him saying that he was dumbfounded by the number of recipients who subsequently thanked him for thanking them![3]

I'm reminded of my late, great friend, Coach John Wooden, the legendary UCLA basketball coach. When people wrote to him, he would always handwrite two-page replies in his beautiful penmanship. He'd include an autographed poster of his Pyramid of Success; then he'd walk the letter to the corner mailbox. His commitment to influencing others left a deep imprint on me. He understood how people hunger for a positive influence.

Another man who has been a great influence on my life for more than a quarter century is Orlando businessman Jimmy Hewitt. He envisioned an NBA franchise in Orlando even before I did, and if it weren't for his vision, energy, and influence, the Orlando Magic would not exist today. From the time he first brought me to Orlando for a speaking engagement, Jimmy has done nothing but build me up and make me believe that I'm one of the greatest sports executives in the world!

When we were trying to turn the Orlando Magic *dream* into a living, breathing *team*, Jimmy kept saying, "We're gonna get this team in Orlando because we've got Pat Williams! No one can say no to us now!" I was able to perform far beyond my true capabilities because of the incredible impact and influence of Jimmy Hewitt.

Pay It Forward

I've listed a few of the people who have truly shaped my life. Now I ask you: Who are the influencers in *your* life? Who are the people who have impacted you in a positive way? Who are the people who have shaped your values and your character? Who enabled you to believe in yourself? Who taught you the ropes of your profession?

You can never pay those people back—and they wouldn't want you to. Instead, they would tell you to "pay it forward" to the people—especially the young people—in your own sphere of influence. So now the question is: *Who are you going to impact with your influence today?*

Leadership guru John Maxwell tells us that the average person influences the lives of around 10,000 people over the course of a lifetime—whether that influence is for good or ill.[4] It's amazing to think that you and I have that kind of impact on the people around us. We all make a difference in the lives of others. The only question is: What kind of difference do we choose to make?

Rick Warren, in *The Purpose Driven Life*, puts it this way: "At some point in your life you must decide whether you want to impress people or influence people. You can impress people from a distance, but you must get close to influence them, and when you do that, they will be able to see your flaws."[5]

It's true: The greater your influence, the more visible your flaws. And that's okay! You don't have to be perfect to impact lives with your influence. In fact, one of the most important ways you can have a positive influence on the people around you is by being transparent and honest about your mistakes and sins. The most important influence we have on people is not through our perfection, but through the example we set in dealing with—and recovering from—our failures.

In the late 1970s, United Technologies Corporation ran a series of thought-provoking ads in the *Wall Street Journal*, including an ad with the headline "Do You Remember Your First Break?" The text under the headline read:

Someone saw something in you once.

That's partly why you are where you are today.

It could have been a thoughtful parent, a perceptive teacher, a demanding drill sergeant, an appreciative employer, or just a friend who dug down in his pocket and came up with a few bucks.

Whoever it was had the kindness and the foresight to bet on your future.

Those are two beautiful qualities that separate the human being from the orangutan.

In the next 24 hours, take 10 minutes to write a grateful note to the person that helped you.

You'll keep a wonderful friendship alive.

Matter of fact, take another 10 minutes to give somebody else a break.

Who knows?

Someday you might get a nice letter.

It could be one of the most gratifying messages you ever read.[6]

Who gave you your first break? Who was your influencer, encourager, and cheerleader? Who impacted your life for the better? Who helped you become the person you are today?

Don't you want to be that kind of person in someone's life today? Don't you want to influence scores or hundreds or thousands of people for the better? I know you do.

Now let's examine some ways to make that happen. . . .

Questions for Group Discussion or Individual Reflection

Chapter 1: The Influences That Have Shaped Your Life

1. Who were some of the most influential people in your life? How have these people helped make you who you are today?

2. Recall some words of insight, encouragement, or advice that someone said to you that continue to affect your life today. Who said those words to you? What were the circumstances? Why did those words affect you so profoundly? Do you think that person would remember saying that to you?

3. Have you ever had a "Mom Burgher" in your life—someone you could talk to when you were a young person? Or a "Bill Durney," someone who mentored you in your career? Or a "Mr. Littlejohn," someone you could always turn to for encouragement, advice, and spiritual wisdom? Or a "Bill Veeck," someone who was a role model and fount of success wisdom? Or a "Phil Frye," someone who would warn you about life's pitfalls and help you keep your perspective in times of stress and pressure? Or a "Rich DeVos," someone who was your "cheerleader" through tough times?

   Maybe there was someone in your life who influenced you in a totally different way. If so, who was that person and how did he or she impact your life?

4. Is there someone in your life right now who needs your influence and encouragement? What steps could you take right now to make a difference in that person's life?

5. Is there someone who impacted your life—someone whose day would be brightened by a note of thanks or a phone call? Make a commitment to write that note or make that call within the next twenty-four hours.

2

Everyone Has Influence

> We all have different spheres of influence. Mine happens to be playing baseball. Wherever you find yourself, you have a sphere of influence and a chance to use your life and gifts for something great.
>
> Southpaw pitcher Clayton Kershaw[1]

During a recent visit to the office of Dr. Yasser Khaled, my myeloma and stem cell transplant specialist, I met one of Dr. Khaled's young assistants, Abraham Toner. He said, "I want to tell you my Charles Barkley story. My dad is from Philly, and we have always rooted for Philadelphia teams. When I was about ten, the 76ers were on the road, playing at Denver. My dad got tickets, and we drove from Wyoming to Denver to see the game. I had brought all my Charles Barkley memorabilia to get them signed if I got the chance.

"The 76ers lost to the Nuggets that night. After the game, the 76ers bus was standing outside the Denver Arena, and my dad and I and the rest of our family waited as the players came out and walked past a line of fans to the bus.

39

"Finally, Charles Barkley came out. He walked right by everybody. The fans were holding out things for him to sign, and he shook his head and said he wasn't going to sign anything. That's when my father did something I'll never forget.

"Dad shouted, 'Charles! I brought my family all the way down from Wyoming! The least you can do is sign a few things for my kid!'

"I just cringed. I thought this was going to be the end of my dad's life. But Charles just kept going past us and got up on the bus. A few minutes went by—I guess he was sitting on the bus, thinking about what my dad had said. Finally, Charles came back out of the bus, sat down on a step in the stairwell of the bus, and he beckoned me over. I went over to him, and he signed all my stuff. He didn't sign for anybody else. As soon as he finished signing, he turned around and got back on the bus, and they left for the airport.

"I still have all of that memorabilia to this day. After that event, I had a whole new respect for my father, in the way he challenged Charles Barkley. And I had a new respect for Charles Barkley. The team had lost and he didn't feel like being anybody's hero that night, but he heard my dad and thought it over, and he signed my stuff."

Charles Barkley has been criticized throughout his career for claiming that athletes should not be held up as role models. He once pointed out that a million guys in jail can dunk a basketball—but should they be role models?[2] In 1993, he wrote his own text for a Nike commercial, in which he said, "I am not a role model. I'm not paid to be a role model. I am paid to wreak havoc upon the basketball court. Parents should be role models. Just because I dunk a basketball doesn't mean I should raise your kids."[3] Though Barkley's claim that he is not a role model was controversial, his advice that "parents should be role models" is certainly true.

Yet I believe the observation of another NBA star, Karl Malone, is equally true. Addressing Charles Barkley through a column for *Sports Illustrated*, Malone said, "I don't think it's your decision to make. We don't choose to be role models, we are chosen. Our only choice is whether to be a good role model or a bad one."[4]

Both Barkley and Malone make good points. Parents should be the primary role models and influences in a child's life—but athletes and other leaders in our culture also have a responsibility to be aware of the influence they wield. Along with fame, wealth, and power come responsibility. Athletes and other celebrities are going to be role models—that's inescapable. But they have a choice between wielding *healthy* influence or *corrosive* influence.

Writer Ray Robinson, in an article for the National Baseball Hall of Fame's *Memories and Dreams* magazine, recalled one of his childhood baseball heroes, the "patrician pitcher," Herb Pennock:

> Victorious in five World Series contests without ever losing one, he surely qualified to be my hero. In paying obeisance, I had also put together an entire scrapbook devoted to him, full of stories, pictures, and his autograph.
>
> However, in later years, when Pennock had become general manager of the Philadelphia Phillies, he took an unconscionable stand against the Brooklyn Dodgers' Jackie Robinson [the player who broke baseball's color barrier], when Robinson was scheduled to play in Philadelphia for the first time. When Pennock threatened to pull his team off the field, it diminished him in my eyes and forced me to re-think how I had felt about him as a youngster.[5]

People are *impressed* by athletic ability but they are *influenced* by the way we treat other people. It takes a lot more than athletic ability to be a hero and a role model. You've got to have good character, good values, and a good heart in order to be someone worth admiring and emulating. A "hero" with great athletic talent but a small mind and a closed heart is unworthy of anyone's adulation.

A Stellar Influence

We all tend to underrate the influence we have with others. Our words and actions have more impact than we realize. You don't have to be an NBA star or a rock star or a four-star general to have a stellar influence on your family, friends, and colleagues. You don't have to be famous or educated to be a role model for others to follow. Influence is a grassroots quality. We all have it—whether we realize it or not.

Six months before Dr. Martin Luther King Jr. was assassinated, he spoke to a student assembly at Barratt Junior High School in Philadelphia. He called those young people to live lives of influence, no matter whether they lived their lives as leaders or as street sweepers. He said:

> And when you discover what you will be in your life, set out to do it as if God Almighty called you at this particular moment in history to do it. Don't just set out to do a good job. Set out to do such a good job that the living, the dead, or the unborn couldn't do it any better.
>
> If it falls your lot to be a street sweeper, sweep streets like Michelangelo painted pictures, sweep streets like Beethoven composed music, sweep streets like Leontyne Price sings before the Metropolitan Opera. Sweep streets like Shakespeare wrote poetry. Sweep streets so well that all the hosts of heaven and earth will have to pause and say: Here lived a great street sweeper who swept his job well.[6]

College basketball coach Rob Evans once shared with me the story of a janitor who was one of the great influences in Rob's life. That janitor was Rob's own father. "When I was eight," he said, "Dad worked for a janitorial service and cleaned lawyers' offices. My three brothers, ages nine, ten, and twelve, and I helped him clean at night. One night, while we were cleaning up in an office, the attorney and a few of his friends came in.

"The attorney was a bullying kind of guy who liked to push people around. He said to my dad, 'Oscar, get over here.' My dad just kept cleaning. The attorney said, 'Get over here now or you're fired!' My dad set his office keys on the desk and said to the four of us, 'Come on boys, let's go.'

"When we were outside, I asked my dad, 'How can you quit this job? Don't we need the money?'

"He said, 'Son, your dignity and your integrity are non-negotiable.' He wanted me to know that no amount of money was worth compromising your human self-worth. That was an important lesson. The attorney tried to demean my father, but Dad maintained absolute control and dignity. He looked big in my eyes, and the attorney, who thought he was such a big shot, looked small. That was a huge lesson for me in what it means to maintain your character and integrity at a high personal cost."

Buck O'Neil was a first baseman and manager in the Negro American League, who played most of his career with the Kansas City Monarchs. Not long before he died, Buck told me that, in spite of limited schooling opportunities for African Americans in the Jim Crow era, he had excellent role models and a great teacher.

"My parents and grandmother taught me about character," Buck said. "They told me, 'Your character will be with you all your life.' When we moved to Sarasota, I met a lady named Emma Booker, who ran the Booker Grammar School, and she had a big influence on my life. She taught character and the difference between right and wrong to all her students. She often said, 'They might be able to segregate you, but they can't segregate your character.'"

Buck said that his father, mother, and Mrs. Booker laid the foundation for his entire life through their influence. "So many children today only have one parent," he told me. "They don't have what I had. Kids today need all the help they can get from good people. My mother and father, my teacher and my pastor, all of them wanted me to be the best I could be."

One of the ways Buck's parents and teachers built character in him was through hard work. "I had to do an honest day's work in the schoolroom," he told me. "Then I worked at home.

I was eight or nine years old, and my job was to bring in the water and fill the tubs up so we could do the wash. That was my duty. I felt bad if I couldn't hold up, but I loved to play ball. I'd come in after dark and my mother would say, 'You've got to quit the game earlier so you can get the water in here before dark.'"

After working summers in the celery fields, Buck moved to Jacksonville, lived with relatives, and attended Edward Waters College. In 1937, Buck signed with the Memphis Red Sox for a year, then went on to play for the Monarchs for the remainder of his long career. "In the Negro Leagues," he told me, "there were so many good ballplayers who wanted to take your job away. There's always going to be competition out there. You've got to have the courage to stay in there. I'm grateful for the role models I had who taught me courage and persistence."

I was saddened in February 2006 when Buck O'Neil, at age ninety-four, was rejected for induction into the Baseball Hall of Fame. But I was proud of the character he displayed—character that was shaped by his parents and by Mrs. Emma Booker. On the night the Hall of Fame vote was announced, he was surrounded by about two hundred friends and family members for what was supposed to be a celebration. When the crowd heard that he had missed being inducted by just one vote, the mood turned somber.

Buck got up, flashed a broad smile, and said, "God's been good to me. They didn't think Buck was good enough to be in the Hall of Fame. That's the way they thought about it and that's the way it is, so we're going to live with that. Now, if I'm a Hall of Famer for you, that's all right with me. Just keep loving old Buck. Don't weep for Buck. . . . Here I am, the grandson of a slave. And here the whole world was excited about whether I was going into the Hall of Fame or not. . . . I couldn't attend Sarasota High School. That hurt. I couldn't attend the University of Florida. That hurt. But not going into the Hall of Fame, that ain't going to hurt me that much, no. . . . Before, I wouldn't even have a chance. But this time I had that chance. . . . I was on the ballot, man."[7]

Those were words of character and influence—and they were part of Buck O'Neil's legacy. The character traits he learned from his parents and Mrs. Booker are embodied in those words. In October 2006, Buck O'Neil passed away. He was born into a segregated world, yet he made his own opportunities with a ball and a bat, faith in God, and an optimistic attitude. If he can accomplish so much after starting with so little, what excuse do any of us have for accomplishing so little when we've been given so much?

Becoming Aware of Our Influence

In January 2012, Christian author and artist Joni Eareckson Tada spoke at my church in Orlando. Before a crowd of five thousand people, she told her story. "In July 1967, when I was seventeen years old," she said, "I did something really stupid. I was swimming in the Chesapeake Bay. I was young and uninhibited, and I swam out to a float in the bay. I got up on that float and dove into shallow water. I suffered a spinal fracture, my spinal cord was severed, and I was paralyzed from the shoulders down.

"That was forty-five years ago, and I've been in a wheelchair ever since. I prayed and asked God to heal me. When that didn't happen, I thought, 'Lord, you'll never be able to use me. I'll never have any influence for you in the condition I'm in.' If you had told me forty-five years ago that I would be speaking all over the world, that I'd have a worldwide radio broadcast, that I'd have written many books, and would have the opportunity to touch millions of lives as a result of my weakness, I never would have believed it. Because of what most people would call a tragedy, I've had an influence that I never would have had if I had remained normal and healthy."

Then she had a special word for people who are handicapped or limited in some way. "Let me just point out to you that you are not on the shelf. You can have a greater impact on people's lives than ever before. Never take yourself out of the game.

God hasn't. He wants to use you right where you are. There's no limit to what God can accomplish through your weakness. I'm living proof of that."

During the writing of this book, I had a conversation with my longtime friend Ernie Accorsi. His long career as an NFL executive includes a decade-long run as general manager of the New York Giants. In the course of our conversation, I said, "I was watching a football game with my grandkids this past weekend, and a Viagra commercial came on. I sat there in dread that one them was going to say, 'What are they talking about, Pops? If *what* lasts more than four hours?'"

"Reminds me of a story from when I was with the Giants," Ernie said. "One year, we didn't have the ad space on the scoreboard sold—this was at the old stadium in the Meadowlands. Finally, the marketing team sold the space to Viagra. So John Mara, as chief operating officer, went to his dad, Wellington Mara [then-owner of the Giants]. John said, 'Dad, we just sold the scoreboard to Viagra.' Wellington said, 'No, son, we're not going to do that.' John said, 'But the scoreboard will be unsold!' Wellington said, 'Then it will be unsold this year.'"

Most people think only of money and how to get more of it. Wellington Mara thought about his influence and the influence of the New York Giants. He thought about the impact of his influence on young fans.

Golf legend Arnold Palmer quit smoking partly for health reasons and partly because he realized that his smoking impacted his image and influence on others. In a 2000 interview with *Golf Digest*, he said,

> I quit smoking on the golf course 38 years ago, [and quit smoking completely] 30 years ago. . . . When I see some of the old film clips and see how silly I am with that thing hanging out of my mouth, how obnoxious I looked, I could just cringe. My father tried to convince me of that when I was younger, but like all kids, I knew more than he did. Fortunately, I could see and feel for myself what those things were doing to me. I can run now at 70 better than I did 40 years ago, when I huffed and puffed.[8]

Another golf legend, Jack Nicklaus, tells a similar story in his 2002 book, *Golf & Life*:

> I smoked cigarettes like many other young golfers. In fact, I was earning money from one of the top tobacco companies through an endorsement deal my manager had negotiated when I turned pro.
>
> While I was watching movie highlights of my first US Open victory, I saw myself on the 13th hole at Oakmont surveying a putt for a birdie with a cigarette dangling from my lips. I threw it down to putt and then picked it up and stuck it in my mouth and left it dangling there as I tapped in my second putt and walked off the green.
>
> As I watched this, I was appalled. "That's just terrible," I told myself. "Here you are, the national champion, which for kids makes you a role model, and there you are, doing just about the most unathletic thing a person can do—and it's going to go down in history on that film."
>
> I felt so strongly about it, I phoned my manager and insisted on canceling the endorsement deal and giving back the money.[9]

The impact of influence begins with an *awareness* of our influence. The greater our awareness, the greater our influence.

I think it's safe to say that the most influential woman in America over the past two decades has been Oprah Winfrey. In 1996, she wondered aloud why a certain potato chip company didn't make their low-fat baked chips with ridges—and within a few months, low-fat chips with ridges were on store shelves. She has inspired and encouraged millions by sharing her personal story of being born in poverty, surviving rape and the death of a baby she gave birth to at age fourteen, and going on to build a successful, influential life.

Some years back, a story on Oprah in *People* magazine demonstrated in a moving way how she became aware of the power of her influence on the lives of her fans:

> A poor single mother from the Chicago area trudged over to that city's Hyatt Regency hotel for the much-publicized 1994

charity auction of Oprah Winfrey's hand-me-down clothes. She was looking for a shred of hope among the cast-off Armanis and Valentinos, but all she could afford was a $5 pair of size 10 shoes that fit like boats on her size 7 feet. Later, she met her idol after an Oprah taping and confessed, "Sometimes I go in the closet when I'm feeling down and I stand in your shoes." Winfrey . . . is quiet for a heartbeat. "That story makes me want to weep," she says. "It makes me think I must be doing something right."[10]

All around us, there are people who would like to be in our shoes, who look to us as role models and influencers in their lives. They are watching what we do, listening to what we say, and following where we walk. Are we aware of the influence we have? Are we using our influence wisely?

Accepting the Responsibility of Influence

In July 1993, I played in the Charles Barkley Celebrity Golf Tournament at a Disney hotel property in Orlando. Also playing in the tournament: basketball legend Michael Jordan. Michael is an intense competitor—and a needler. He loves to offer his wry commentary on your swing, your putt, and your chances of ever getting out of that bunker. And wouldn't you know it—Michael's foursome was right behind mine.

We came to the thirteenth hole, a tough par three, shooting from a hill downwards over some water. Our group had to wait for the foursome ahead of us—and soon, Michael's foursome, surrounded by a gaggle of media people with TV cameras and microphones, descended on us. I groaned inwardly. I hadn't hit the ball solidly all day—and there I was, teeing up under the watchful eye of Michael Jordan and his vast entourage. The whole time I was warming up and trying to get focused, M. J. was smirking at me.

Lord, I prayed, *if you let me hit this one ball well, I'll be satisfied!*

I planted my feet, visualized a long, sailing drive down the fairway—and I took my swing. The ball flew skyward, a straight, perfect trajectory. There was a hush all around me as everyone watched the gorgeous trajectory of that ball. No one said a word, not even the loquacious Mr. Jordan. The ball settled gently on the green and rolled to within a few feet of the hole.

No one was more astonished than I.

"Hey, Pat," Michael said, breaking the silence, "it's easy to see that you don't spend much time at the office!"

Ah, that little jab was the finest compliment my modest golfing skills have ever received! Never mind that when I got to the green, I totally muffed the putt! The important thing is that, when it really counted, I impressed Michael Jordan!

People of influence are people we respect, people we want to impress. Who wouldn't love to have Michael Jordan say (even in a backhanded way), "Wow! You did great! I'm impressed!"

Michael Jordan is not a perfect human being, but he has truly dedicated himself to living as a positive role model, especially for the young. When our family brought home our seventeenth and eighteenth children, Caroline and Alan from Brazil, I quickly enrolled Alan (who was eight) in a youth basketball program at the Y. His approach to the game was unusual, to say the least. I loved to watch him at the practices.

Alan's playing style resembled soccer as much as basketball. On one possession, Alan got the ball and he dribbled, carried, and drop-kicked the ball toward the basket—then he leaped, fired the ball into the air, and by some miracle known only to the angels, the ball rolled around the rim a few times before falling through the net.

All the way home after the game, Alan bounced up and down in the car, talking a hundred miles an hour in Portuguese, shouting, "Quasi Michael Jordan! Quasi Michael Jordan!" In English that means, "I'm almost Michael Jordan!"

This boy, who a few weeks earlier had been running through the streets of São Paulo, could imagine himself to be the next Michael Jordan. I thought, *Wow! So many kids want to be just like Michael Jordan. That man is a role model with an amazing amount of influence—he has a lot to live up to not only for millions of kids here in America, but for kids around the world!*

Once when my son Richie was a teenager and Michael and the Bulls were in town to play the Magic, I arranged for Richie to be the ball boy. Before the game, I introduced Richie to Michael Jordan. Looking up at Number 23, Richie was speechless. At moments like that, many players will shake a young person's hand or sign an autograph. Michael went even further. He put his arm around Richie and shared his philosophy of life.

"Richie," he said, "if you really want to be successful in life, there are three things you must do. First, if you want to do something in life, then *do it*. Don't let anything stand in your way. Set a goal, then stay focused on that goal. Second, whatever you choose to do, work hard at it. Nothing great was ever accomplished without hard work. Third, stay in school. You've got to get it done in the classroom in order to be successful."

Well, Richie was completely wowed by that message. How could a kid *not* be impacted by the influence of those words from the heart of Michael Jordan? Clearly, Jordan is a man who is continually aware of his influence.

Whether you are an NBA superstar or a street sweeper, you have influence. Every word you speak and every action you take has an impact on people, so be continually aware of your impact on others. Take responsibility for your influence. People are watching you all the time. Don't let them down.

In 1981, when I was general manager of the Philadelphia 76ers, I learned that our owner was selling the team to a man named Harold Katz. The deal had been negotiated quietly. I had no idea who Mr. Katz was, or what he looked like. The first time I was introduced to him was mere minutes before the press conference at which he was to be announced as the new owner.

Yet the first time we met, I instantly recognized him. I had shaken his hand dozens of times, completely unaware that he would one day be my boss. You see, Mr. Katz was a 76ers season ticket holder. Many a night, I had stood at one of the gates of our arena, greeting our fans—and one of those fans was Harold Katz.

As we shook hands, I said, "This goes to show that it pays to be nice to your season ticket holders. You never know when one of them might own you."

Mr. Katz laughed and agreed—and I worked with him for the next five years.

A Reluctant Young Influencer

About ten years after our Brazilian-born son Alan joined our family, he was attending a Christian high school in the Orlando area. Alan was full of enthusiasm, friendly and outgoing, and well-liked by his peers. Alan only had one problem in school—but it was a big one: He was a cut-up. He loved to talk in class, make jokes, and get attention—and the result was that he was frequently a disruptive influence on his fellow students.

I received an average of three or four calls a week from the school, asking me to deal with the latest problem behavior Alan had unleashed. I had to sit him down again and again and say, "Alan, you need to be aware of the influence you have on your fellow students. Your teachers and your principal tell me that the other kids look up to you and follow your lead. Alan, we all want you to be a leader, and to do that, you need to be more responsible. We know you can be a leader and a role model if you put your mind to it."

But that argument did not get through to Alan. He understood that a leader can't be a cut-up. A role model can't be disruptive. A person of influence must set a good example for the rest of the class. But Alan didn't want any of that. He just wanted to have fun. I didn't know what we were going to do.

One day, Alan came home bursting with exciting news. "Guess what?" he said. "My coach wants to make me captain of the basketball team!"

"Hey, that's terrific, Alan!" I said. "Do you know what this means?"

"No. What does it mean, Dad?"

"What do you have to do to be captain of the team? You have to lead. You have to be a role model and set a good example. You have to use your influence wisely."

"You mean," he squeaked, "I'm a leader?"

"That's right, Alan. You're a leader."

Being captain of the basketball team definitely produced a change in Alan. No, the calls from school didn't stop altogether. Alan was still Alan. But thanks to his new leadership role, Alan became much more aware of his influence—and he began to accept responsibility for his impact on others. Everybody has influence—even a teenager who would rather be the class cut-up!

How will you use your influence today?

Questions for Group Discussion or Individual Reflection

Chapter 2: Everyone Has Influence

1. Describe your sphere of influence. How many people do you think you influence (or are capable of influencing) in any given day?

2. What are some ways that you could be more conscious, aware, and deliberate about influencing other people in a positive way? What are some ways you could motivate yourself to live in an influential way?

3. What are some specific *actions* you could take today or tomorrow to impact another person's life in a positive way? What are some specific things you could *say* to have an impact on others? Are there any practical or mental barriers that hold you back from doing and saying the things that would positively influence others? (For example, is the person you want to influence unpleasant

and unapproachable? Are you held back by shyness or not knowing what to say?) How might you overcome these barriers?

4. Suppose you had never been born. How would the lives of people around you be changed if you did not exist?

   What does this tell you about your own influence? How does it affect the way you view yourself? Does it change the way you want to live your life from now on? If so, how?

5. Buck O'Neil said, "So many children today only have one parent. They don't have what I had. Kids today need all the help they can get from good people." How can you have a positive impact on the lives of children around you—in your family, your church, or your neighborhood?

3

Healthy Influence

Serving, Mentoring, and Empowerment

> Granger turned to Montag. "Grandfather's been
> dead for all these years, but if you lifted my skull . . .
> in the convolutions of my brain you'd find the big
> ridges of his thumbprint. He touched me."
>
> Ray Bradbury, *Fahrenheit 451*[1]

*I*n 2009, *The Sporting News* assembled a blue-ribbon panel of
Hall of Fame players and coaches to rank the Fifty Greatest
Coaches of all time, in all sports. The panel's number one
pick: John Wooden, legendary head coach of the UCLA Bruins.
His unmatched record of ten NCAA national championships
over twelve years will probably never be equaled. In the decades
following his retirement, his former players—Kareem Abdul-
Jabbar, Gail Goodrich, Walt Hazzard, Andy Hill, Bill Walton,
and many others—made frequent pilgrimages to his Encino,
California, home to seek his wisdom and thank him for his
impact on their lives.

I became personally acquainted with Coach Wooden in the final decade of his life while writing two books about him, *How to Be Like Coach Wooden* and *Coach Wooden: The 7 Principles That Shaped His Life and Will Change Yours*. But I first became aware of him in 1962, when I was a senior at Wake Forest. That year, our basketball team, with Len Chappell, Billy Packer, and Coach Bones McKinney, advanced to the Final Four. That was also the first year Coach Wooden's Bruins made it to the Final Four.

Wake Forest lost to Ohio State in the national semifinal, then defeated Coach Wooden's Bruins in the consolation game. That game was significant because it was Coach Wooden's last NCAA tournament loss for a very long time. Over the next dozen years, Coach became the winningest coach in college basketball history, amassing ten NCAA championships, 88 consecutive wins, and 38 consecutive NCAA tournament victories.

After becoming personally acquainted with Coach Wooden, I eagerly looked forward to my visits with him. I wanted to soak up every atom of his influence, his wisdom, his values, his faith, his stories, his advice, and the aura of his personality. I wanted to be more like him. Though I was in my sixties when I first spoke with him face-to-face, I actually feel like he taught me, coached me, and mentored me—and I wanted him to be proud of me. I wanted him to know how much his influence meant to me, and how deeply he impacted my life.

Coach Wooden and I lived a continent apart, yet he became an integral part of my life. I read books by and about Coach Wooden, and I memorized his maxims (known as "Woodenisms"). Above all, I wanted to influence the lives of others in the same way he impacted my life and hundreds of other lives.

After Coach Wooden retired, someone asked him the one thing he truly missed about coaching. "I'm a teacher," he replied, "and I miss teaching the young men." When he said "teaching," he was talking about influence.

After Coach Wooden passed away at age ninety-nine, one of his most famous players, Kareem Abdul-Jabbar, wrote a tribute to Coach in *Los Angeles* magazine, reflecting:

> Those of us lucky enough to be coached by him, will remember him not just as a great coach who changed basketball but as a great man who changed our lives. He didn't just teach us how to be the best athletes, he taught us how to become the best men we could be.
>
> His genius as a coach and mentor lies in the fact that we were hardly aware that these valuable life lessons were being taught. We didn't realize that all the drills and all the practices and all the instruction were preparing us for the most important part of our lives—the part that came after basketball. . . .
>
> Hardly a day goes by that I don't think about Coach Wooden's influence on me.[2]

That's the kind of influence Coach John Wooden had on his players, his assistants, his fans—and yes, that's the kind of healthy, positive influence he had on a veteran sports executive named Pat Williams.

There are three powerful forms of healthy influence that are available to us all, regardless of whether we live in the limelight or the shadows, whether our deeds will appear in the record books or go unnoticed by the world at large. We can all be servants. We can all be mentors. We can all be empowerers. Serving, mentoring, and empowering are three ways to impact others with our healthy influence.

The Influence of Serving

Dr. Dan Gerdes is author of two books, *Through the Storm* and *Coaching for Character*. When I interviewed him a few years ago, he told me that we who seek to influence the next generation should use our influence "not to gratify or satisfy the self, but to serve others. As teachers and coaches, we need to instill in young people the image of leading as a form of serving. When I played basketball in college, that was what my coaches told me: Leadership means sacrifice. It's doing all sorts of things that nobody sees, nobody notices, and nobody thanks you for. It's being a servant."

This vision of influencing-by-serving was given to us by the apostle Paul in the New Testament:

> Each of you should look not only to your own interests, but also to the interests of others.
> Your attitude should be the same as that of Christ Jesus:
>
> > Who, being in very nature God,
> > did not consider equality with God something to be grasped,
> > but made himself nothing,
> > taking the very nature of a servant,
> > being made in human likeness.
> > And being found in appearance as a man,
> > he humbled himself
> > and became obedient to death—
> > even death on a cross!
>
> Philippians 2:4–8

In the fall of 1976, when I was general manager of the Philadelphia 76ers, I helped arrange the deal that brought "Dr. J," the legendary Julius Erving, to our team. Doc brought a new style of play to the game, making big plays above the rim (including his signature "slam dunk"), while introducing the crossover dribble and no-look pass.

Despite his stature in the game, his stats, and his championship rings, Doc is a humble servant who lives to influence others. In 1980, when the 76ers negotiated a new contract for him, I asked Doc to do a basketball clinic at a Christian camp in Schroon Lake, New York. I told him the camp couldn't afford to pay him—and Doc said, "Don't worry about it. I'm glad to do it for free."

In July 1981, I went to Albany to meet his flight and accompany him to the camp. When Doc arrived, I learned that he had just come from another basketball camp in Colorado and he hadn't slept more than three or four hours. We took a boat to the island where a thousand kids had gathered for the basketball clinic. The camp had a huge welcome prepared for Doc, with a band, a parade, streamers and flags, and a cheering crowd.

It was a hot summer day and I could tell that Doc was tired—yet he threw himself into the camp, gave the kids all he had, was patient and kind, and impacted those kids with his influence in ways they would never forget. After the clinic, I drove Doc back to the airport and thanked him profusely for all he had done—volunteering to be a servant to those kids, asking nothing in return. He humbly waved off my thanks, said it was his privilege, then boarded the plane and took off for home.

The following summer, August 1982, I joined an entourage that included Doc, his wife, Turquoise, and five other NBA players for a two-week trip through mainland China. It was a fabulous adventure through an exotic land, but we also saw a lot of poverty and sadness. Dr. J was at the height of his career, and everywhere he went, people wanted to pamper him—but Doc didn't want to be pampered.

In the city of Han, the ancient capital of China, we stayed in a guesthouse in the country. The facilities were primitive but there was one very nice room which was reserved for Doc and his wife. We had a group meeting before bedtime and Doc shared that he was not comfortable having the best room in the house. He didn't want any special treatment. Clearly, Doc preferred to serve others rather than to be served.

Another story about Dr. J comes from John Gabriel, a good friend. "It was in the days before charter flights," Gabriel told me. "The team got up the next morning after winning the 1983 NBA championship, and the players boarded the hotel minivan for the drive to the airport. Julius got aboard and sat in the first available seat, putting his arm around the twenty-three-year-old video coordinator next to him. 'Gabe,' Doc said, 'you did a fantastic job this season!' That young video coordinator was me. Doc's words of encouragement have stayed with me all these years. I've never forgotten his kindness."

Who You Are When No One Is Looking

I've noticed that people in the service industry—limo drivers and wait staff in particular—can easily tell you about servants.

A lady named Pam was my driver in Chicago a few years back. She told me about picking up Debbie Reynolds and her entourage of musicians and dancers at O'Hare Airport. Pam found the entire group of entertainers waiting around the baggage carousel because their luggage had gotten waylaid—and they were in for a long wait.

"Miss Reynolds and her people could have made a big fuss about being inconvenienced," Pam said, "but they decided to make the best of the situation. They broke out in song and they danced and did some comedy routines right there at the luggage carousel. They attracted quite a crowd, got a lot of applause, and had a chance to publicize their upcoming show."

I received a fascinating glimpse into a great serving heart when I was in Chicago for a speaking engagement. My limo driver was named Jim, and the person who stood out in his memory was singer Ray Charles. "I drove Ray Charles around Chicago for the day," he said, "and the next day I took him to the airport for a morning flight to Pittsburgh. He asked me about my family, and I told him I had a brother in Pittsburgh who is blind. Ray, being blind himself, was intrigued and asked me questions about my brother, including how to contact him. I didn't expect anything to come of that, but later I got a call from my brother. He was all excited and said, 'Guess who I had lunch with today!' I said, 'Umm, Ray Charles?' That shocked my brother. 'How did you know?' So I told him about our conversation. It turned out that after Ray arrived in Pittsburgh, the first thing he did was go straight to my brother's house and take him out to lunch. I'll never forget that."

One of the names I hear most frequently when I talk to limo drivers is that of General Colin Powell. A few years ago, I spoke at a seminar in Philadelphia. My driver was Joel Richman. He said, "When I told General Powell that I had served in Vietnam, he talked to me as if we were blood brothers. His respect and concern for me were genuine. He wanted to know how I was doing and if there was anything I needed. Even though I was no longer in the service, it was as if he was still looking out for his troops."

Years later, I flew to Cincinnati for a speaking engagement and my driver, Bob Ward, told me another story about General Powell. "He arrived in a private plane at a small airport near Cincinnati," Bob told me. "He got into the car and said, 'Before we go to the hotel, I need to stop at a place called the Sherman House.' I had never heard of it, so I called my dispatcher for directions. The dispatcher checked and said, 'It's in a really bad neighborhood.'

"But General Powell insisted we go. It turned out to be a group housing facility for homeless veterans. I went in with General Powell, and he spoke for about twenty minutes to the veterans who lived there. He showed them a good time, and they had a lot of laughs. At the end of it all, the general thanked them for their service. I could tell it had been quite a while since a lot of those guys had heard one of their countrymen say, 'Thank you.'

"Then I drove him to his hotel. General Powell was in Cincinnati to give a corporate speech—but I think, in his mind, going to Sherman House and serving those homeless vets was his real reason for being in Cincinnati."

There are few people who have had greater influence and a greater impact on history than Mohandas Gandhi. He led the drive for the independence of India and pioneered the use of nonviolent resistance as a means of fighting for civil rights and freedom. His example inspired many civil rights leaders who came after him—Martin Luther King Jr., Nelson Mandela, Steve Biko, and Benigno Aquino Jr., to name a few.

While campaigning to liberate India from British rule, Gandhi never sought power. He simply identified with the most powerless people of his country. When he traveled by train, he booked third-class passage, which meant being crammed into cattle cars in miserable conditions of heat, filth, and stench. When someone asked Gandhi why he traveled third class, he gave a humble servant's reply: "Because there is no fourth class."

If you want to have influence with others, become a servant. Find a person with windows that need cleaning—then clean them. Find someone whose lawn needs mowing—then manicure it. Find someone who is friendless—and be a friend. Read to a child. Serve meals at the homeless shelter.

Do you want to be a person of influence? Then be a servant.

The Influence of Mentoring

I attended my fifty-year high school reunion in October 2008. Tower Hill School was a fairly small private school in Wilmington, Delaware. Though we were missing some old friends, a lot of the 1958 graduating class was there. We held a Saturday-night banquet at a country club near Wilmington, and the event organizers asked me to emcee.

At one point in the evening, I asked the group, "Of all the Tower Hill faculty, which teacher impacted your life the most?"

We went around the room, and the answers amazed me. Though a number of different teachers were named, there were two teachers who were recalled by almost every alumnus in attendance: Miss Buckles, the seventh grade English teacher, and Mr. Oviatt, the twelfth grade English teacher.

Miss Buckles and Mr. Oviatt were full of energy and enthusiasm—and they made it *fun* to study English. Sure, they could be demanding and they set high standards, but everyone who had studied under these two teachers now looked back over a span of half a century and said, "They had a lasting impact on my life. I would not be where I am today if not for Miss Buckles and Mr. Oviatt."

I particularly remember Mr. Oviatt's inventive ways to make an impression on his students. If you turned in an essay, and he thought you were writing meaningless filler, he'd draw a broken shovel in the margin (this was to suggest that you were slinging so much bovine fertilizer that you had busted your shovel). He also walked around the room with a sawed-off baseball bat—not as a threat, but as his personal trademark. Everyone knew he was a nice guy, but he liked to convey a tough-guy image. No one feared Mr. Oviatt or his bat. We respected and loved him because he was a great teacher.

Miss Buckles and Mr. Oviatt weren't just teachers—they were mentors. They took time with every student. If you had a school problem or a personal problem, you could go to them for insight and a sympathetic ear. Many of my classmates kept in touch with Miss Buckles and Mr. Oviatt for decades after graduation.

Many people mistakenly view mentoring as a micro-influence—"merely" impacting one life at a time. But look at what Miss Buckles and Mr. Oviatt achieved through mentoring. They touched the lives of every person in that room at a very deep and life-changing level. Multiply *that* impact by all the years they served at Tower Hill School, then multiply *that* impact by the influence all of their students had on other people around *them*. You quickly begin to see how the impact of mentoring radiates out, making a powerful difference in countless lives.

Though I have tended over the years to see various coaches, players, and owners as my career mentors, on that night in October 2008, listening to story after story of the impact of these two teachers, I realized Miss Buckles and Mr. Oviatt were definitely two of the key people in my own life. They laid the academic foundation for my second career as a speaker and author.

As this book was being written, the *New York Times* published a front-page story about a study conducted by researchers from Harvard and Columbia—a study that tracked 2.5 million students over a twenty-year period. By isolating and removing all extraneous factors, the researchers were able to identify poor, average, and excellent teachers, then study the impact of these teachers on their students over the long term. They analyzed the students' lives in terms of whether they went on to college, their level of earnings, the age at which they had children, and other outcomes. "The results were striking," said the *Times*, concluding that students taught by "top teachers" were "less likely to become pregnant as teenagers, more likely to enroll in college, and more likely to earn more money as adults."

These findings have far-reaching significance for both individual students and for society as a whole. The researchers found that replacing a poor teacher with merely an average teacher would raise the lifetime earnings of a single classroom by $266,000. To put it another way, a poor teacher can *drag down* the lifetime earnings of a classroom of students by more than a quarter of a million dollars. One of the study's co-authors, Professor John N. Friedman, concluded, "If you leave a low value-added teacher in your school for 10 years . . . you are hypothetically talking about $2.5 million in lost income."[3]

It would be fair to say that great teachers and mentors who truly shape lives as Miss Buckles and Mr. Oviatt did would add an equivalent amount of value to students' lives, to our society, and to our economy. Great teachers and mentors also influence students to stay in school, finish college, avoid teen pregnancy, and live more satisfying and socially responsible lives.

Education policy researcher Eric A. Hanushek, a senior fellow at the Hoover Institution at Stanford, concludes, "Everybody believes that teacher quality is very, very important. What this paper and other work has shown is that it's probably more important than people think . . . [and that the] differences between really good and really bad teachers have lifelong impacts on children."[4]

The classroom is not the only place we need mentors and influencers. We need mentors in our churches, sports teams, businesses, military bases, youth clubs, neighborhoods, and homes. Young entrepreneurs, executives, scientists, doctors, writers, musicians, artists, athletes, teachers, preachers, and public speakers all need mentors.

Even firemen need mentors. Battalion Chief John Salka has served with the Fire Department of New York for more than three decades, and is a mentor, trainer, and public speaker. In his book *First In, Last Out*, Salka writes:

> What is mentoring anyway? It's one of those terms that gets thrown around a lot, and I think everyone has an idea of what it means, but I've encountered few people who could confidently define it. Mentoring . . . is simply teaching and transparency. It means allowing someone to assume the role of student, and then answering his questions and letting him observe how you do your job. It means explaining things using a context he's familiar with. . . . *Mentoring* is really a fancy word for teaching.[5]

To be a mentor, you simply need to have acquired some knowledge, wisdom, and good character in your journey through life. You need to be willing to devote yourself to influencing others through close, personal, one-on-one teaching relationships. You need to care about people, and you need to be able to critique people fairly and objectively. You need to be willing to commit time to other people, to listen to them, to instruct them, and to hold them accountable.

The greatest example of mentoring the world has ever known was Jesus of Nazareth. He spent large amounts of time with His twelve closest disciples, both as a group and as individuals. He built relationships with them and communicated His vision to them. He knew each one as an individual. He knew their strengths and weaknesses, their hopes and fears, their talents and deficiencies. Through a process of building a close relationship with each of the twelve, He was able to shape their character and impart such character traits as courage, integrity, perseverance, and humility. As a mentor, Jesus knew His disciples so well that He could:

- predict Simon Peter's defection and restoration;
- nickname James and John the "sons of thunder" because of their tempestuous personalities;
- count on the energy and enthusiasm of Simon the Zealot;
- recognize the character qualities in Matthew, even though he was a tax collector and a social outcast; and
- tap into the rough-hewn strength of Andrew and the other three illiterate fishermen.

Jesus mentored each one of them in a distinct and individual way. He not only taught them and imparted knowledge to them, but He affirmed them, built their confidence, and challenged them to sharpen their skills. He provoked their thinking by asking open-ended questions. He sent them out into challenging situations where they could stretch themselves and learn by doing. He cheered their successes and helped them learn from their mistakes and failures.

One of the most important tasks in the mentoring process is delegating authority to the disciple, so that he or she learns by doing. Early in His ministry, Jesus preached, taught, healed, and cast out demons. Later, He sent His disciples out to preach, teach, heal, and cast out demons in His name. This is His model of influencing by mentoring:

First, Jesus says to the disciples, "I'll work; you watch."

Next, He says to them, "I'll work; you help."

Then, He places still more responsibility on them, saying, "You work; I'll help."

Finally, He entrusts the work to them, "You work; I'll watch."

That is how to influence people through the impact of mentoring.

The Influence of Empowerment

Longtime major league baseball manager Sparky Anderson was a good friend of mine for more than four decades. He once shared with me an incident from a spring training game against the Red Sox in Winter Haven, Florida.

During batting practice before the game, a man walked up to Sparky to shake his hand. "Hi, Sparky," the man said. "I'm Ted Williams."

Well, of course Sparky Anderson knew Ted Williams—one of the greatest players in the history of baseball. "Ted," Sparky said, "that's funny! As if *you* ever needed an introduction! You never have to introduce yourself to anyone—and least of all to me."

"Oh yes, I do, Sparky," Williams explained. "It can't be any other way. I would never want you to be embarrassed if you happened to forget who I was."

Sparky concluded by saying, "Now that is a man with class! He introduced himself to make sure that *I* wouldn't be embarrassed! Ever since Ted introduced himself that day, I've tried to follow his example. Whenever I meet somebody, I always put my hand out and say, 'Hi, I'm Sparky Anderson.' It's not a big deal—but it makes the other person feel important. If it makes other people feel good, why not do it?"

Ted Williams and Sparky Anderson lived to empower others by helping people feel good about themselves and building their confidence. Ted and Sparky had a lot of influence in the sports world, and they used it to have a healthy impact on players and fans. That's the influence of empowerment.

Another word for empowerment is *edification*. To edify means to *build someone up*. The term comes from the same root as *edifice*, a building. If we want to impact others with our influence, we need to build them up. Unfortunately, all too many people are better at tearing others down than building them up.

Paul "Bear" Bryant, longtime football coach of the Alabama Crimson Tide, recalled how his mentor and football coach, Frank Thomas, empowered him to believe in himself as a player:

I'll never forget, we were going out for the 1935 Rose Bowl game. I went into the men's lounge on the train. Coach Thomas was sitting there with some of the coaches and Red Heard, the athletic director of LSU, and two or three newspapermen. He said, "Red, this is my best football player. This is the best player on my team." Well, shoot, I could have gone right out the top. I mean, he didn't have to say anything else. I know now what he was doing, because I try to do it myself. He was getting me ready. And I was, too. I would have gone out there and killed myself for Alabama that day.[6]

One of the best ways to empower others is to *offer praise and encouragement at strategic times.* We shouldn't simply scatter empty praise all the time, because people see through that—empty praise is quickly recognized as an empty gesture. But a well-timed word of affirmation, a thumbs-up, a smile and a nod, or a pat on the back can provide a high-octane jolt of influence to someone who looks up to us.

If you really want to impact someone with your influence and empowerment, give that word of praise in the form of a handwritten note. (And no, an email is just not the same.) Why should we praise people in writing? It's because a handwritten note can be treasured, read again and again, and can even be suitable for framing. Uplifting words have much more impact when they are written on a card or on personalized stationery.

Another principle of empowerment is *always praise in public and criticize in private.* When Chuck Daly was head coach of the Orlando Magic, he told me about a lesson he learned when he was an assistant to Vic Bubas, head basketball coach at Duke University in the 1960s: "Vic taught me to bite my tongue. He said, 'You have to know when to talk to players and when to keep your peace.' Vic taught me to always ask myself: 'Will this player benefit from what I say? Or will he just become less coachable?' Sometimes I would literally jam my knuckles in my mouth or look someplace else—anything to keep from saying what I was thinking."

I was general manager of the Philadelphia 76ers when Harold Katz took over as our new owner. Harold was always eager to improve attendance at our games. One time, I came to him with an idea for a new promotion—God and Country Night. It was a flag-waving celebration of patriotism, and the event drew a sell-out crowd. The following day, Mr. Katz called me into his office, shook my hand, and said, "Brilliant promotion, Pat! I'm as proud of you as if you were my own son!"

Those words of empowerment really fired me up! I was walking six inches off the ground as I left his office. I went back to my desk and began cooking up more ideas. Two weeks later, I tried another promotion—and it fell flatter than a steamrolled tortilla. Not only did that promotion *not* draw the fans to the arena, I think it actually frightened fans away.

The next morning, Harold Katz called me into his office—and this time he was livid. "What kind of lame-brained idea was that, Williams? That's got to be the worst 'promotion' in the history of professional sports! I'm taking this out of your paycheck!"

Well, he couldn't actually take it out of my paycheck—but he really wanted to. I thought my job was in jeopardy—and from then on, I hesitated to take on any creative risks. Whenever I brainstormed ideas, I felt Mr. Katz breathing down my neck—and I decided to play it safe.

If you want to impact people and empower them to take creative risks and dare to attempt great things, then build them up, don't tear them down. If they fail, pick them up and help them believe in themselves again. I've always tried to remember that lesson whenever people have disappointed me.

When you make a point of influencing others by encouraging and empowering them, you'll soon find that empowerment flows both ways. On several occasions, I was in the audience when a young woman named Lisette Dolby gave a powerful, persuasive speech on behalf of the Salvation Army. When she spoke, you couldn't help but be impacted by her warmth and sincerity. After one such speech, I went up to her, introduced myself, and told her I thought she was a very persuasive speaker with a bright future. I encouraged her to keep "wowing" audiences the way she "wowed" me. A few days later, I received this note:

Dear Mr. Williams—

I'll never forget your words of encouragement after my presentation at the United Way Victory Dinner. Because of your encouragement, I have decided to pursue continued opportunities to "wow" folks and I am working on several new presentations.

Thank you!

Lisette Dolby

Well, after reading that note, I felt empowered! When you influence others by empowering them to believe in themselves, you'll often find that empowerment flows back to you.

Newscaster David Brinkley, whose broadcast career spanned more than five decades, described how the encouragement of one of his high school teachers became the foundation for his career:

A world turned for me in Mrs. Burrows Smith's English class at New Hanover High School. When I wrote a few pages of something and showed it to her, she actually read it, commented on it, told me what she thought and when it was good she said so. When it was not good, she told me what was wrong and how to improve it. After some months, she said to me, "David, I think you ought to be a journalist."

It was the first time that idea had ever occurred to me.[7]

If you want to impact people with your influence and empowerment, praise their efforts. Celebrate their successes, and don't wait. Some words need to be said at just the right moment—and when that moment passes, it's too late. Seize the moment and offer the words of influence and empowerment that people are longing to hear.

I once spoke at a breakfast in the city of Washington in western Pennsylvania. Dwayne Durham rode with me on the drive to the Pittsburgh airport for my flight back to Orlando. Dwayne had been a Pennsylvania state trooper for twenty-five years before taking early retirement at age fifty-two. I asked him why he retired so young. "There was lots of stress on the job," he said, "not from the public, but from upstairs. I discovered that one 'you bonehead, you messed up' can wipe out ten 'attaboys.'"

It's true. Discouraging, disempowering words are incredibly destructive. As people of influence, we need to continually find new and creative ways to enable people to have confidence in themselves. There are many ways to say it: "Well done!" "You keep topping yourself!" "Couldn't do it without you!" Better yet, find concrete, specific actions and character qualities to affirm and praise: "The way you persevered through those obstacles challenged us all to work harder." "I was impressed by the way you remained calm and professional when dealing with that irate customer." "I've seen the way you lead the Bible study in your youth group, and I foresee an exciting future for you in Christian leadership."

Coach John Wooden would tell his players, "Whenever you score, point to the player who set up that score with a pass or screen." Sometimes a player might ask, "What if he's not looking?" Coach would reply, "He'll be looking—I guarantee it!"

We all look for encouragement and empowerment. Whenever we empower the people around us, we set them up for success. Empowerment is an elixir for the soul.

In May 2011, four months after I was diagnosed with multiple myeloma, I attended the Dick Vitale Gala for Cancer Research in Sarasota, Florida. Dick hosts that event every year to raise funds for the V Foundation, which was founded to honor the late Jimmy Valvano. It's a huge event, and there were over a thousand people attending—all of Dick's basketball buddies, players, coaches, and media personalities. Lovely FOX News broadcaster Erin Andrews (who was with ESPN at the time) was the emcee for the evening.

I had never met Erin. Erin called me to the platform and said, "Pat Williams is the co-founder of the Orlando Magic, and he's fighting a battle with cancer himself. We're all praying for you, Pat." And she said some other kind things about me, then finished with, "Let's give him a nice welcome!"

The audience applauded and I really felt a spiritual and emotional surge from Erin's words and the applause in the room. It was like medicine to my soul.

It was a great evening, and after it was over and the people were leaving, I saw Erin in the middle of the ballroom, talking to a couple of college coaches. I walked over, waited for a break in the conversation, then said, "Erin, thank you so much for the kind things you said earlier this evening. You and the audience really lifted my spirits tonight."

Her eyes lit up and she said, "Oh, Pat, we're all thinking of you and praying for you. Hang in there and be tough, and remember all the people who are pulling for you to beat this thing."

Every time I see Erin on TV, I think of her kindness—and her empowering words.

While this book was being written, I had lunch with Rita Brown and her daughter, Jenn Brown. Rita is prominent in the world of international gymnastics, and she's involved with the gymnastics section of the International Olympic Committee. Jenn is an analyst for ESPN—you've probably seen her doing sideline reports at Thursday night football games.

Attractive and talented, Jenn has enjoyed a meteoric rise at ESPN. She's also a person of faith and strong convictions, and she wanted to know if there wasn't more that she could be doing with her media platform to have a healthy influence on others. She wondered if there might be a way to have a greater impact outside the realm of sportscasting.

I said, "Jenn, I don't think you realize the impact you have on people right where you are on ESPN. The sports world is a world of influence. Just imagine for a moment, if all of the sports in our country and across the world were to shut down—if there were no more professional sports, no more college sports, no more Olympics, no more youth sports, if the whole world of sports just vanished. Can you imagine what our country would be like? As a result of what you are doing on TV, you've got an incredible platform, a position of influence that very few young women have. You are impacting lives. Let me tell you about one of your colleagues who's had a great impact on me."

Then I shared with her how Erin Andrews had impacted my life at the event in Sarasota. "Jenn," I said, "Erin Andrews has probably long forgotten that evening and the words she said—but I will *never* forget. That was eight months ago, and here I am, telling you about it now. Jenn, you can have an enormous impact and influence on people everywhere you go."

During our conversation—almost as if I had arranged it—a young waitress came over and said to Jenn, "I recognize you! You're that reporter on ESPN! You're wonderful! Just seeing you on TV inspires me to believe that I might be able to do exciting things with my life, too! I just had to come tell you what an inspiration you are."

Jenn thanked her and gave her some well-chosen words of encouragement. As the waitress departed, I gave Jenn one of those "See there?" looks. That's all that needed to be said—

About the influence of empowerment.

It Doesn't Take Much

If you want to have a healthy influence on others and a positive impact on the world, focus on these three forms of influence: servanthood, mentoring, and empowerment. You don't need fame or wealth or power to have influence. You don't need to be a captain of industry or a great philosopher, with a long list of degrees after your name. You simply have to be yourself. You simply have to be willing to serve others, to mentor others, and to empower others. Serving, mentoring, and empowering are three practical ways that anyone can impact other people with a healthy, positive influence.

On June 2, 1949, baseball history was made at Shibe Park in Philadelphia. In a game against the Cincinnati Reds, the Phillies hit a record five home runs in the eighth inning. Del Ennis, Willie Jones, and Schoolboy Rowe each hit one homer in that inning, and my boyhood idol Andy Seminick hit two homers. The Phillies won that day, 12 to 3, and that game went into the history books. To this day, every June second, sportswriters across the country recall the day the Phillies hit five homers in one inning.

Andy Seminick passed away in 2004, but he used to live in Melbourne, Florida, not far from Orlando. One June day in the early 1990s, I took him out to lunch just to congratulate him and reminisce. "Andy," I said, "I just wanted to tell you that your name was in all the papers across America today, celebrating your greatest day in baseball."

He smiled, and I could see the memories stirring behind his eyes. "Thanks, Pat."

"Andy, what is your most vivid memory of that game?"

I expected him to talk about the pitch, or what the count was, or his emotions as he faced two Reds pitchers that day, Ken Raffensberger and Kent Peterson. But he didn't mention any of that.

"My most vivid memory," Andy said, "is that the next day, I came to the ballpark and went to my locker—and there on my locker was a handwritten note from Mr. Carpenter, the owner of the Phillies. I remember it word for word. He wrote, 'Congratulations, Andy. I'm proud of you. You did a great job.' That's what I remember most vividly about that game."

It didn't take much time or effort for Mr. Carpenter to write that note to Andy Seminick, but what a profound impact it made. Forty-plus years later, that note was Andy's most vivid recollection of the greatest accomplishment of his career. With that one note, Mr. Carpenter served, mentored, and empowered Andy Seminick.

How can you have a healthy influence on someone today?

Questions for Group Discussion or Individual Reflection

Chapter 3: Healthy Influence: Serving, Mentoring, and Empowerment

1. Describe a time when you did something for another person without wanting anything in return—a time when you simply wanted to have a positive influence on someone else? How did that turn out? How did you feel afterward?

2. When you hear the word *servant*, what picture pops into your mind? Is there someone in your life who exemplifies servanthood? Give some specific examples of ways this person has served you or someone else.

3. Who has been a mentor in your life? What impact did this mentor have on your thinking and your direction in life?

4. Have you ever been a mentor to anyone else? Are you mentoring someone now? What are some of the problems and difficulties of mentoring someone? What are some of the joys and rewards of mentoring someone?

5. What does the word *empowerment* mean to you? Name one or two people who have been significant empowerers in your life. What steps can you take this week to become a more effective empowerer of others?

4

Character: *The Key to Influence*

> I believe that it is not only my right, but my duty to
> use my influence for the betterment of the world in
> which I live, and that my influence depends upon
> my personality and the opportunity to express my
> character.
>
> Newspaperwoman and suffragette Ida Clyde
> Clarke, "My Suffrage Creed," 1910[1]

*B*obby Jones was an outstanding player for the Philadelphia
76ers during my tenure there as general manager. He was
not only a great defender and an ambidextrous shooter,
but also a strong Christian leader and a man of great integrity
and influence. He was intense on the court, yet humble and
self-effacing off the court.

One of the first things Bobby did when he joined the Sixers
was to come to me with a plan to hold a chapel service before
Sunday afternoon games. I thought it was a terrific idea, and
we began holding team chapels almost immediately. Only three
players showed up at our first chapel—Bobby and Julius Erving

77

from the Sixers and a Milwaukee player, Kent Benson. But from that small and inauspicious start, the concept of team chapels quickly spread throughout the NBA, and into the NFL and major league baseball as well.

That's just one example of the character of Bobby Jones. Here's another:

One night, we were playing in San Antonio. Bobby raced toward the sideline after a loose ball that went out of bounds. The referee's view was blocked, so he said, "Bobby! Did you touch that ball?"

"No, sir," Bobby said, "I didn't."

The ref said, "Sixers' ball."

A week or so later, we were playing a home game at the Spectrum Arena in Philadelphia. The same referee was assigned to the game. Once again, the ball headed out of bounds and Bobby reached for it. Just as before, the ref's view was blocked.

"Bobby," the ref called out, "did you touch that ball?"

"Yes, sir, I did."

So the ball went to the other team.

The Sixers coach, Billy Cunningham, stomped his foot and said, "Bobby! Let the referees call the game!"

Bobby replied, "I can't compromise my integrity over one call."

Here was a young man who cared intensely about winning—but he cared even more about his integrity and influence. There are few players who could be trusted to make an honest call on themselves—but the refs knew that they could always get the truth from Bobby Jones. His influence was rooted in his uncompromising character.

Character is the key to influence.

How We Build Character

Influence is the ability to change hearts and minds through the way we live our lives. Therefore, *character is influence*. If you lack character, you are incapable of genuine influence. If you have a depth of good character, you *can't help* but positively impact the people around you. Your influence naturally flows from your character like fresh water from a good spring.

People watch you all the time. Your children notice when you break the speed limit or sneak office supplies home from work. Your employees notice when you fudge your business ethics or lie to customers. Your co-workers notice when you cheat on your expense account.

You are continually influencing the people around you for better or worse. So live your life as if you are under a microscope, even in your private moments. Make sure there is no glimmer of daylight between your words and your actions. If you guard your character and practice seamless integrity, you'll have an enduring influence.

I would define *character* as "who we are when we are tested by temptation or adversity." It's easy to be honest when there is no temptation to lie or steal. It's easy to talk about courage when there is no danger, no pressure, and nothing at risk. It's easy to be "generous" and give millions to charity when we have a few billion in the bank. It doesn't take any character to do what comes easily. We need character for the difficult tests of life, for times when we are under stress or facing a difficult moral choice.

Some people define *character* as "what you do when nobody is looking," and that's true. If you have such strong character that you consistently choose to do the *right* thing even when you could get away with doing the *wrong* thing, that is character indeed. But character also means doing the right thing when people *are* watching you, pressuring you, and trying to get you to go along with them. Standing up to peer pressure and taking a strong moral stand is also an unmistakable sign of character.

We build character by the choices we make. Every time we resist temptation, or stand firm under pressure, or give of ourselves in a selfless way, our character grows stronger. The next time we are put in a position of testing or temptation, it will be easier to do the right thing because we have begun making a habit of character-based decisions. In the same way, weak character is the result of habitually making easy choices—yielding to temptation, taking the easy way out, going along with peer pressure, and so forth. For good or ill, character is the result of the choices we make and the habits we acquire over time.

Some of the qualities that make up good character include perseverance, personal accountability, courage, honesty, integrity, humility, self-control, and generosity. Let's take a closer look at a few of these character qualities and ask ourselves: Have I built these qualities into my own character? How does my strong character (or my defective character) impact my influence on others? What do I need to do to become more persistent and persevering? How can I become more consistently honest? How can I prepare myself to take a stronger stand against peer pressure?

Let's take a survey of some of the qualities that make up your character and mine. First, let's look at the character quality of *perseverance*.

Dr. George Yancey is associate professor of sociology at the University of North Texas and the author of such books as *Beyond Black and White* and *Beyond Racial Gridlock*. He told me how he learned an important lesson in perseverance when he was in high school.

"I was pretty skinny in high school," he said, "and not a very good football player. But I played high school football until my senior year. During a practice in the off-season, the coaches taught us a new drill. It was odd, because it didn't seem to have anything to do with football.

"Two players stand on a mat and grab a towel with both hands. Then we were to fight until one person took the towel away from the other person. We couldn't hit or kick the other person, but everything else was fair game. The coaches picked me to be the first person to try it, and they matched me with a guy who was a least ten pounds bigger than me. We each grabbed the end of the towel. The coach blew the whistle, and the guy started slinging me all over the place. I couldn't keep my footing, but I held on for dear life. I was determined not to let go of that towel—I refused to quit.

"Finally, after what seemed like ten minutes of struggle (but was really less than one minute), I could tell that my opponent was getting tired of throwing me around. We were down on the mat, and I managed to jerk the towel from one of his hands. I wrapped my legs around his other arm and pulled with my entire body—and finally yanked the towel free. At that moment, the whistle blew. The coach seemed surprised when he saw I had taken the towel from the other guy.

"After my turn, I watched the other players fight for the towel. I was amazed to see that no other player won the drill outright. No other player was able to take the towel away—I was the only one.

"I realized later that the purpose of the drill was to see how hard we would fight and how long we would persevere. It was designed to test and strengthen our competitiveness. The coaches didn't expect anyone to win—and that's why the coach looked so surprised when I actually won. I'm glad I didn't know that. If I had known the coaches didn't expect any of us to win, I might not have fought hard enough to take the towel—and I wouldn't have learned a valuable lesson in perseverance. I found out I could accomplish whatever I needed to if I would keep fighting—if I fully believed that failure is not an option. That lesson in perseverance has served me well in life."

The character trait of persistence or perseverance is essential to any great achievement. As the apostle Paul writes, "So let's not allow ourselves to get fatigued doing good. At the right time we will harvest a good crop if we don't give up, or quit" (Galatians 6:9, THE MESSAGE).

The late, great Alabama football coach, Paul "Bear" Bryant, believed that character is as great an indicator of future success as athletic ability. He understood that *character is influence* for good or ill—and that one player who lacked the character trait of perseverance could, through his negative influence, cause an entire team to quit on itself. He said, "There's one thing about quitters you have to guard against—they are contagious. If one boy goes, the chances are he'll take somebody with him, and you don't want that. So when [players] would start acting that way, I used to pack them up and get them out, or embarrass them, or do something to turn them around." Bear Bryant also observed, "The first time you quit, it's hard. The second time, it gets easier. The third time, you don't even have to think about it."[2]

Personal accountability is another essential to our influence. Marilyn Carlson Nelson, chair and CEO of Carlson Companies, told me how she learned an important lesson in personal responsibility and accountability:

"When I was young," she told me, "our family always went to church together on Sunday. I was in seventh grade and still attended Sunday school classes instead of the adult worship service. Sometimes the classes were chaotic, with kids talking and shooting spitballs and little or no order maintained. One Sunday, I announced on the ride home that I wasn't going to Sunday school anymore. It was a waste of time, I said, and I'd rather go to the sanctuary with the adults and hear the sermon each week.

"I thought my dad and mom would praise my decision. Instead, my father pulled off the highway, stopped the car, and turned around to look at me. He said, 'You *what*?' I repeated my very mature reasoning for not going back to Sunday school.

"He looked at me sternly and said, 'If the Sunday school isn't working, then *change* it.' There I was, only thirteen years old, and my father was ordering me to fix a Sunday school class in a huge downtown church—a class that even the adult teachers were not able to control!

"I started to cry. My mother tried to intercede with my father, but without success. In fact, he suggested that she call the Sunday school superintendent and set up a meeting so that I could present my ideas for 'fixing' the Sunday school class.

"So I went home and wrote down a list of ideas for improving the Sunday school class. My mother made the appointment. The day came, she drove me downtown, and we had the meeting. And you know what? The superintendent was *happy* to hear my ideas. He instituted the changes I had suggested, and we fixed the Sunday school.

"I learned that if I think something needs to be changed, I shouldn't expect someone else to do it. It's my responsibility to take action and change it. Throughout my adult life and my career, I have often thought back to that lesson, and it has guided me to this day."

Another character trait essential to our influence is *honesty*. Golf is a character sport. No other sport prizes honor, honesty, and personal integrity more than the sport of golf. A golfer is expected to own up to his own faults. In April 2010 at Hilton Head Island, South Carolina, British golfer Brian Davis was on his way to winning his first PGA tour victory at the Verizon Heritage tournament. As regulation play ended, Davis was tied with American golfer Jim Furyk. On the first playoff hole, Davis's approach shot landed off the green and nestled into a patch of weeds. While wedging the ball onto the green, Davis thought he heard a faint *tick* in his backswing, as if the club had grazed a stalk of grass. PGA rules impose a two-stroke penalty if your club moves any impediment (even a blade of grass) during the backswing.

Davis asked the PGA officials to check the TV replay and see if any tall grass was disturbed by his backswing. The officials looked—and they saw a reed of grass move ever so slightly. The motion was so faint it could only be seen in slow-motion—and no one would have caught it if Davis hadn't requested the replay.

Brian Davis's honesty cost him the win—and an additional $411,000 in prize money. But he gained an enormous amount of influence. Tournament director Slugger White later said of Davis, "He's class, first class." Davis's actions won him countless admirers as that crucial moment was replayed again and again on sports channels and news shows around the world. He showed that in golf, as in life, the way you live your life and guard your influence is even more important than winning.[3]

What is the lesson of this incident for you and me? Simply this: When we make a mistake of any kind, we need to honestly admit it for the sake of our influence. The willingness to acknowledge our own faults is a major (and much overlooked) aspect of honesty. Leadership experts James M. Kouzes and Barry Z. Posner remind us:

> Nothing undermines or erodes your credibility and your effectiveness as a role model faster than not being willing to acknowledge and take responsibility when you've made a mistake. . . .
>
> When you ask people what it means . . . to be honest, their immediate response is that "she tells the truth" or that "he doesn't lie." The more reflective response—and crucial insight—is: "They're willing to admit when they are wrong. I know that they are capable of being honest with me when they say they made a mistake." Think about that. If you want others to perceive you as being honest, it's not just about telling the truth when it's easy. The more revealing test is telling the truth when it's difficult, even embarrassing and possibly damaging, to do so. Admitting you're wrong or that you don't know are some of the best signs that a leader can be believed.[4]

Character begins with a decision. Whenever we make a decision, we need to consider how that decision will impact our influence on others. We need to think of all the people who look up to us—then ask ourselves, "How will *they* be affected by my actions, my choices, and my character?"

We can influence others through our character in amazingly simple ways. I once interviewed Dr. Roy E. Yarbrough, director of sports management studies at the California University of Pennsylvania. He told me, "I demonstrate my character to my students by being on-time for class, by responding to student email within twelve hours, by learning my students' names, and by taking time to listen to them. These sound like simple, inconsequential acts, but I've found that these small actions give me credibility and influence with my students. My life is under scrutiny, and I have to prove my character by the way I live.

"Some of my senior students have told me, 'I've been in college four years and you're the only professor who knows my name.' Why should that be? It's so easy to take note of a student and to have an influence on that young person's life. My goal is not only to impart knowledge, but to instill character. One of the easiest yet most effective ways to do that is by showing students you care about them as people."

"You'll Never Lie, Will You?"

Courage leads to influence—especially the courage to take a lonely stand against peer pressure. Dave Hart, athletics director at the University of Tennessee, shared a story with me that perfectly illustrates the courage to stand alone. "My parents taught me my core values," he said. "One time in elementary school, I gave an answer in class. The teacher encouraged the class to debate whether I had given the right answer or not. Some of my classmates agreed with my answer, some did not. As the discussion continued, the teacher suggested arguments against my answer. The longer he talked, the more he influenced the class to reject my answer. If a student spoke up to support me, the teacher would suggest that he or she might want to give it a bit more thought.

"One by one, all of my supporters went over to the opposite position. No one in the class agreed with me. The teacher turned to me and said, 'Mr. Hart, would you like to change your answer?'

"I was tempted to abandon my answer—but I didn't. I said, 'No. I'm not going to change my answer.'

"The teacher said, 'Why not? Everyone in the class agrees you're wrong.'

"'I still think I'm right.'

"The teacher turned to the class and said, 'Mr. Hart *is* right. He stood firm against popular opinion. I was able to persuade the rest of you that he was wrong.' He proceeded to apply the lesson of that exercise. He said we needed to think for ourselves and make the right choice, even if the whole world is against us and says we're wrong."

It was a lesson in courage and influence that Dave Hart never forgot. The teacher demonstrated how corrosive influence works—including the corrosive influence of peer pressure. And Dave Hart demonstrated the impact of healthy influence by standing for what he knew was right, even though he had to stand alone.

To be a man or woman of influence, you must have the courage to endure conflict, criticism, and opposition while standing for your values and beliefs. As Max Lucado once observed, "A man who wants to lead the orchestra must turn his back on the crowd." People of influence often stand alone.

As people of influence we also need uncompromising *honesty*. Michael Reagan, son of the late President Reagan, tells a revealing story about honesty and integrity in his book *The New Reagan Revolution*. It takes place in 1965, before Reagan had ever held political office. Justin Dart, head of the Rexall Drugstore chain, invited Reagan to his corporate office to discuss the possibility of a gubernatorial run. An extremely wealthy man, Dart was influential in political and business circles and was in a position to raise huge amounts of money to fund a political race.

Near the end of their conversation, Dart pointed to a paper sack. "That's for you," he said.

Reagan lifted an eyebrow. "What's in it?"

"Open it up and see."

Reagan opened the sack and found it filled with cash—$40,000.

Justin Dart said, "It's a little something for you and Nancy."

Ronald Reagan closed the sack and hurled it at the drugstore executive. "Do you think that if I win the governorship, you're going to own me?" he asked angrily. "I don't want to be governor that much. In fact, I've changed my mind. If that's what being governor is all about, I don't want the job."

And Reagan stamped out.

A few days later, Justin Dart was able to set up a second meeting—and this time he began with an apology for even suggesting that Reagan could be bought.

Ronald Reagan accepted Dart's apology, then laid down some conditions: He would run for governor, but if he was elected, he would not owe any special favors. Justin Dart would have no more access to the governor's office than any other citizen.

"I understand," Dart replied—then he added, "I've never met a politician like you. *They all take the money.*"[5]

Isn't that a sad commentary on our political system? They all take the money. If you want to maintain your influence in the world, you have to be one of those few who stand out from the rest—one of the character people, one of the honest people, one of those few people who would *not* take the money, but would instead throw it back in anger.

Another key character trait when it comes to maintaining our influence is *self-control*. My longtime friend Bobby Richardson was a second baseman for the New York Yankees from 1955 to 1966. He's an outspoken Christian, who is a leader in the Fellowship of Christian Athletes. Though Bobby is happy to share his faith with anyone who asks, he is always gracious, never pushy or judgmental. He's been invited to share his faith at the White House and at the funerals of Roger Maris and Mickey Mantle.

Around the Yankees clubhouse, Bobby stood out as one of those rare players who never lost his temper and never used profane language. Even though he didn't rebuke anyone else for foul language, he noticed that the other players all seemed to rein in their behavior when he was around. He'd approach a group of players who were telling lewd stories or bragging about their sexual exploits, then one of them would see Bobby and nudge the others—and they'd all stop talking.

"I never meant to spoil anyone's fun," Bobby told me. "I never said they should stop talking that way. I didn't preach at them. They just all seemed to change the subject whenever I came by."

During one game, Bobby and his fellow players were in the dugout at a game, and Moose Skowron struck out. "Moose came back to the bench," Bobby recalled, "and he was cussing and turning the air blue. Oh, he was mad! Then he saw me. He got a guilty look on his face and said, 'Excuse me, Bobby.' Then he walked right on past me, cussing some more! I just had to laugh."

Bobby Richardson is a man of influence because he is a man of self-discipline and self-control. The impact of his influence flows directly from his character.

How to Live, How to Love, How to Die

The late tennis champion Arthur Ashe won three Grand Slam titles and was the first African American selected to the United States Davis Cup team. Following a heart attack in 1979, he underwent quadruple bypass surgery, followed by a second open-heart surgery in 1983. During the second surgery, Ashe received a transfusion of AIDS-tainted blood (current blood screening methods have significantly reduced the odds of such an occurrence today). Ashe publicly revealed that he had AIDS in April 1992, and he died the following February, just a few days after completing the manuscript of his memoirs, *Days of Grace*. The book opens with these words:

> If one's reputation is a possession, then of all my possessions, my reputation means most to me. Nothing comes even close to it in importance. Now and then, I have wondered whether my reputation matters too much to me; but I can no more easily renounce my concern with what other people think of me than I can will myself to stop breathing. No matter what I do, or where or when I do it, I feel the eyes of others on me.[6]

Those are the words of a man who is intensely aware of his influence. Ashe also told about an incident that happened when he was seventeen and competing in the Middle Atlantic Junior Championships in Wheeling, West Virginia. The only black player in the under-eighteen section of the tournament, Arthur stayed in a cabin with a number of white players. One night, the other boys trashed the cabin and blamed the damage on Arthur. The incident even made newspaper headlines—and the newspapers seemed to side with the white players against Arthur.

A few days later, young Arthur Ashe rode from Wheeling to Washington, D.C., for another tennis tournament. During the trip, he wondered what his father would say to him about the incident. Immediately upon arriving, Arthur went to a pay phone and called his dad. As Arthur expected, his dad had read about the cabin-trashing incident—and he had just one question to ask:

"All I want to know is, were you mixed up in that mess?"

"No, Daddy," Arthur said, "I wasn't."

Arthur Ashe concludes, "He never asked about it again. He trusted me. With my father, my reputation was solid. . . . I want to be seen as fair and honest, trustworthy, kind, calm, and polite. I want no stain on my character, no blemish on my reputation."[7]

The moral of the story—the moral of Arthur Ashe's entire life—is this: *Always be conscious of the impact of your influence.*

We are under scrutiny at all times, whether we know it or not. All around us, people are watching us, observing how we deal with adversity and opposition, how we respond to temptation, how we make wise decisions, and how we handle unfair criticism. We need to make sure that when people watch our example we never let them down or lead them astray.

When I started my chemo treatments in the winter of 2011, I'd come into the chemo room, sit down in my chair, and quietly receive the treatment without any conversation, without any real expression on my face. I didn't talk to any of the other patients in the room. It was all rather impersonal—and, frankly, depressing.

One day, a nurse took me aside and said to me, "Mr. Williams, all these people in the other chemo chairs know who you are and what you're going through. They're all going through the same thing. So from now on when you come in here, would you do these people a big favor? Would you please go around to each of the other patients, put a smile on your face, and give them a good word? If you would do that before you begin your treatment, I think it would make a big difference in the mood in that room—and it might even aid in everyone's healing process."

I took that nurse's advice, and for the rest of the time that I went to my oncologist's office for chemotherapy, all the way through the summer of 2011, I made a point of greeting my fellow patients. I would high-five them and kibitz with them, and we mutually encouraged each other. I've found that in the process of trying to be a positive influence in that chemo room, I get a lot of positive influence in return. Good influence is good medicine.

I'm so glad I took that nurse's advice. Now, wherever I go, wherever I speak, and even through the pages of this book, I'm doing the same thing I did in that chemo room. I'm trying to be continuously aware that people are watching my example, they're observing how I deal with adversity, and they are looking to me for encouragement and hope. I don't ever want to let them down. I don't want to let *you* down.

I also urge you to teach the impact of character to your children, your students, your subordinates, and to everyone within your sphere of influence. Tape up quotations about character and influence around your home, by the bathroom mirror, or the family computer. Post character quotations around the locker room and the gym, around the classroom, around the church, around the office, or around the barracks. Surround the people you care about with reminders that our influence flows from our character.

Author and publisher Elbert Hubbard often wrote about character and influence. In one of his most famous essays, "The *Titanic*," he wrote about the last moments of those who lost their lives in the 1912 sinking of the *Titanic*, including Macy's department store magnate Isidor Straus and his wife, Ida. Isidor refused to board a lifeboat ahead of the other passengers, and Ida refused to board without her husband—so they voluntarily remained together on the deck of the doomed ship.

In his essay, Hubbard concluded, "Mr. and Mrs. Straus, I envy you that legacy of love and loyalty left to your children and grandchildren. The calm courage that was yours all your long and useful career was your possession in death. You knew how to do three great things—you knew how to live, how to love, and how to die."[8]

Three years after the sinking of the *Titanic*, Elbert Hubbard and his wife Alice booked passage on the ocean liner *Lusitania*, bound from New York to Europe. They planned to gather stories so that they could report back to America on the events of World War I. Six days out of port, a German submarine torpedoed the *Lusitania* without warning.

Ernest Cowper, a survivor of the attack, was carrying a baby to a lifeboat when he saw the Hubbards on the boat deck. They stood arm in arm, gazing out to sea as the ship slowly settled into the Atlantic. Cowper approached them and asked, "What are you going to do?"

Elbert Hubbard shook his head, but said nothing. Alice smiled and replied for both of them: "There doesn't seem to be anything to do."

Then the Hubbards turned, went back to their cabin, and closed the door behind them. They made a decision to lock themselves in their cabin, where the Atlantic waters would not separate them. Like Isidor and Ida Straus, Elbert and Alice Hubbard knew how to live, how to love, and how to die.[9]

The final moments of Isidor and Ida Straus—and of Elbert and Alice Hubbard—were marked by character, courage, and love. In life, they influenced many people. In death, their stories impacted many lives.

If you want your life and death to influence others, then live a life of significance and meaning. Live to impact others with the quality of your character.

Questions for Group Discussion or Individual Reflection

Chapter 4: Character: The Key to Influence

1. The author writes, "Influence is the ability to change hearts and minds through the way we live our lives. Therefore,

character is influence. If you lack character, you are incapable of genuine influence." Yet nobody is perfect and we all make mistakes. How do we grow as people of influence even while we struggle to overcome our weaknesses and character flaws?

2. What is your greatest character strength? What is your worst character weakness? What steps can you take to overcome your weak areas and improve your overall character and integrity?

3. Who supports you, encourages you, prays for you, and holds you accountable for your character growth? What steps can you take this week to find an accountability partner, recovery group, or counselor and begin working seriously on your character issues?

4. If you are a parent, mentor, youth leader, or teacher, what are you doing to model good character and strong values to the young people you influence? What additional steps could you take to have an even more effective influence on their character?

5. Remember the story of golfer Brian Davis who called attention to a blade of grass that was just barely flicked by his golf club: Maintaining his integrity cost him $411,000 in prize money and a tournament win. If you had been in Brian Davis's position, would you have done what he did? Why or why not? Would you have been able to live with the choice you made or would it bother you for years to come? (For example, would you have felt guilty for not calling a fault on yourself? Or would you have felt like a fool for giving up all that prize money because you blew the whistle on yourself over a minor technicality?)

6. Do you think character matters in a leader—or can a person be a great leader without having good character?

5

The Influence of Our Actions

> As our actions will influence others who share a
> single web of social relationships, we must think
> and behave unselfishly.
>
> H. James Birx, *The Encyclopedia of Time*[1]

As I write these words, my second-born son, Bobby Williams, is the manager of the Viera Nationals, a minor league baseball club in the Gulf Coast League. When we moved our family to Orlando, Bobby was an eleven-year-old Little League catcher. One day, I happened to mention Bobby to Boyd Coffie, the baseball coach at Rollins College in Winter Park, near Orlando. Boyd had been a catcher in the Yankees farm system, so when I told him Bobby wanted to be a catcher, Boyd said, "Why don't you bring him over to Rollins this fall? Let him work with our college catchers here. He can do practices and drills with the team. I'll give him a little instruction."

"Boyd, you'd go out of your way like that to help an eleven-year-old boy?"

"Absolutely. Bring him over."

I remember the first day I took Bobby to meet Coach Coffie and the Rollins players. Though Bobby was hungry to learn, he was nervous at the thought of being on the same field with a bunch of college players who were almost twice his age. As we left the house, his anxiety got to him and he started to cry—but his fears were soon dispelled.

The moment we arrived, Boyd made Bobby feel right at home, taking him under his wing, talking man-to-man as if Bobby was one of his varsity players. Every day after school, Bobby would be there at those practice sessions, eager to play ball. It was a thrill for him to play baseball with the varsity players, and to receive pointers and coaching from Boyd himself and from the other catchers.

Boyd Coffie passed away in 2006, but his positive impact on Bobby continues to this day. By the time you read these words, Bobby will have finished his thirteenth year in professional baseball—and much of the credit goes to the actions of Coach Coffie at a formative time in Bobby's life. That experience built Bobby's confidence, honed his skills, grounded him in the fundamentals, and gave him an understanding of the game that was far beyond his years. Though Bobby didn't have enormous success as a player, he became an effective teacher and coach. I'd say that Bobby can teach catching as well as anyone in baseball at any level.

Coach Coffie was a man of influence because he was a man of action. Some coaches would have said, "The last thing I need is an eleven-year-old kid hanging around." But Boyd took the first step, inviting Bobby to come to practices, and taking an active, involved role in influencing Bobby as a player—and as a young man. We all have enormous power to influence others through the impact of our actions.

Influence by Example

In *Christian Reflections on the Leadership Challenge,* James M. Kouzes and Barry Z. Posner talk about the importance of influencing others through our example:

The most powerful thing a leader can do to mobilize others is to set the example by aligning personal actions with shared values. Leaders are measured by the consistency of their deeds and words—by walking the talk. Leaders show up, pay attention, and participate directly in the process of getting extraordinary things done. Leaders take every opportunity to show others by their own example that they are deeply committed to the values and aspirations they espouse.[2]

John C. Onoda is on the advisory board for Fleishman-Hillard International Communications, and has previously held executive positions with the Charles Schwab Corporation, Visa USA, and Levi Strauss. He once said, "I tell top management to think of themselves as actors in a silent movie. No one can hear a word you're saying. You have to communicate completely through your actions. You have no words, only behavior with which to communicate."[3] If your life were a silent movie, if the only way people could learn about your character, your beliefs, and your values was through the actions of your everyday life, what would they learn?

William Lane Craig is a professor of philosophy at the Talbot School of Theology and the author or editor of more than thirty books. Dr. Craig told me his father, Mallory John Craig, set an example of humility and quiet strength through his service in World War II. "My father was a member of 'the greatest generation,'" Dr. Craig told me. "He served in the Eighth Air Corps, based in Britain. He fascinated us kids with stories, photographs, and souvenirs from the War. He was awarded a Bronze Star, but whenever I asked what it was for, he always joked, 'just licking the General's boots.'"

For Dr. Craig, his father's life was a study in influence through action. "He worked a lot around the house," Dr. Craig told me, "and would typically order a few tons of rock or fill dirt, and then begin to chip away at the pile, one wheelbarrow load at a time. The task would look hopeless, but in a few weeks or months, the piles would be gone and a rock wall built or a ravine filled." Their family called this the "turtle method"—a reference to the story of the tortoise and the hare—and Dr. Craig told me that his father's example has been "my inspiration in my work as a Christian scholar. The key to getting things done is just consistent, constant plugging away, bit by bit."

Dr. Craig has fond memories of the time his father spent with the kids—"memories of his playing games with us as kids, taking us on hunts for fossils and geodes, going on train rides, taking me on business trips to Chicago, traveling with me to the New York World's Fair, and so on. He was a railroad man, who rose from a lowly clerk to become a vice president of a spur line of the Santa Fe called the Toledo, Peoria, and Western Railroad. He was uncompromisingly honest. Late in his career, he actually preferred to be overlooked for promotion rather than acquiesce in certain shady practices that were going on. I admired him for his stand, at the expense of his career."

The elder Craig was also involved in local government, serving as chairman of East Peoria's City Planning Commission. "He had to officiate at public hearings at which certain angry citizens would stand up and rail against him," Dr. Craig told me. His father would smile and graciously absorb the anger and abuse. "'Why don't you get those people back?' I asked him in frustration. 'I would have unloaded on them!'" But his father explained that his job was to listen to the people, not argue or correct them. "In my debates with non-Christians on university campuses," Dr. Craig concluded, "I've tried to exhibit the same calmness and graciousness of spirit that my dad exemplified."

Dr. Craig has debated Antony Flew and Christopher Hitchens on the existence of God and the validity of the Christian faith. Antony Flew later moved from an atheist to a deistic position, thanks in part to Dr. William Lane Craig's gracious presentation of the evidence during those debates. It's fascinating to realize that much of Dr. Craig's debating style is actually an echo of his father's grace under fire during those planning commission hearings in East Peoria, so many years ago.

Dr. Bob Paeglow is the founder of Compassion in Action / Koinonia Primary Care, a medical and mental health care ministry to the poor located in Albany, New York. Dr. Paeglow told me how he was challenged and influenced to devote his life to medical ministry by an encounter with a Brazilian man known as Neto. "In 1994, I was a thirty-nine-year-old fourth-year med student at Albany Medical College," Dr. Paeglow told me. "I received a call from my friend Peter. He said, 'Bob, you've got to meet this guy sitting in my office! He's been telling me about what he's been doing in Mozambique.'"

The fifteen-year Mozambique Civil War had ended in 1992, at a cost of more than a million dead from war and starvation. Many survivors suffered wounds from land mines and other weapons of the brutal slaughter. At Peter's urging, Bob Paeglow met with the Brazilian man, Sebastiao "Neto" Veloso, who was raising money and recruiting volunteers to take medical supplies and equipment to outfit a cholera hospital for refugees in central Mozambique.

"Neto had a smile that could light up a room," Dr. Paeglow recalled. "We met and talked, and within an hour, we were close friends. Neto had given up a lucrative career in Brazil to follow his heart to Mozambique. He was engaged to be married in four months, and his fiancée gave him an ultimatum—'It's either me or Africa,' she said. Neto told her, 'I love you, but I have to follow my calling to Africa. Come with me.' In reply, she took off the engagement ring and threw it at his feet. Neto picked up the ring and sold it to buy a plane ticket to Africa."

Four months later, Bob and Peter were at the Albany County Airport, ready to take off and join Neto on his mercy mission to Mozambique. The ticket agent asked how many bags they were checking. Bob replied, "Twelve." At first, the ticket agent refused to allow them to check twelve bags, citing airline regulations. But after Bob and Peter insisted that the agent check with higher-ups, an airline vice president ordered the ticket agent to help them load their twelve bags on the plane. Soon, they were on their way to Mozambique—a land of incredible suffering.

"We worked in seven refugee camps," Dr. Paeglow told me, "with fifty thousand refugees in various stages of disease and starvation. In our makeshift clinic, we encountered every conceivable horror. There were cases of malaria and infection, topped with lice and scabies. Peter and I would return from a long day in the clinic, after seeing hundreds of people, and we'd flop onto our mattresses on the floor and cry until our pillows were soaked with tears."

One day a traffic collision not far from the clinic left nine people severely injured. Bob Paeglow and Peter operated through the night using only local anesthetics. After treating only half the patients, they ran out of anesthetics. For the rest of the patients, the two men had to cut flesh and stitch up wounds, hoping their patients were in too much shock to feel the scalpel. Every crash victim survived.

Shortly before Bob and Peter were to return to the States, Neto Veloso organized a special church service to thank them. During the service in a thatched-roof, mud-walled church building, Neto called the two men forward. Neither Bob nor Peter knew what would happen next. "Now it's our turn to give to those who have given so much to us," Neto said. "Come forward and bring your offering of thanks to God for them!"

The Mozambican parishioners came up in a line and placed their offerings on a mud altar at the front of the church. One bent old woman placed a single hen's egg on the altar. A one-legged man on a makeshift crutch (who had lost the other leg to a land mine) brought a single small coin. The people filed past, placing a banana, a sweet potato, or a coin on the altar. Bob and Peter wept openly as the procession passed by.

When the coins were counted, they totaled thirty-three cents. "It was too holy to ever spend," Dr. Paeglow told me. "The coins remain in our office to this day—a gift from the poorest of the poor."

The experience Bob Paeglow had in Mozambique, thanks to the influence of a Brazilian man named Neto, convinced him to dedicate his life to ministering to the poor. He has gone on more than twenty overseas medical missions, and he operates his clinic in the poorest section of Albany, New York. Sometimes people ask him why he has devoted his life to serving the poor instead of using his medical skills to make a more comfortable living. He replies that the thirty-three cents he received from the poor in Mozambique is a far richer payment than any millions he might earn as a doctor to the rich.

In the summer of 1997, Dr. Paeglow learned that Neto Veloso had died in Mozambique of unknown causes at age thirty-two, giving his life for the Mozambican people. He was buried in a shallow grave in central Mozambique. In a tribute to Neto on his website, Dr. Paeglow wrote, "Thank you for introducing me to the world of caring for the least, the last, and the lost! Rest in God's arms until we meet again."[4]

Everyone eventually dies. But those who sacrifice themselves to influence others will live on in the lives and actions of others. As long as Dr. Bob Paeglow continues to serve the poor, Neto Veloso's influence lives on as well.

Leading by Example

My friend Bobby Bowden coached the Florida State Seminoles football team from 1976 to 2009, retiring with a career record of 377–129–4. In 1991, when sportswriter Ben Brown was writing a book about the Seminoles football program, he told Bobby he planned to call the book *Saint Bobby and the Barbarians*. A devout Christian, Bobby was horrified, and thought that "Saint Bobby" sounded sacrilegious. "No," he told Brown, "I don't think it's wise to call me that."

"Well," Brown said, "this is what we want to do."

So Bobby called his pastor and asked him if it was sacrilegious for Brown to refer to him that way. The pastor replied, "No, all early Christians were called saints."

Bobby went back to Brown and okayed the title. "But I had to check it out with my preacher first," Bobby recalled.[5] As always, he was thinking first and foremost about his influence and the example he set for others.

Bob Antion assisted Bobby Bowden in the 1970s, when Bobby coached the West Virginia University Mountaineers, and he shared his story with me. Antion, a Penn State grad, arrived at West Virginia in 1974, hoping to land a position as a grad assistant. By the time he arrived, the positions were all filled.

"Coach Bowden told me I could be a dorm counselor until a position opened up," Antion told me. "That was fine with me. I moved into the dorm early, and started going to fall football practice. Soon the rest of the counselors arrived on campus, and the head counselor invited me to attend a 'welcome back picnic.' I understood the picnic to be optional, so I skipped the picnic in favor of football practice.

"The next morning, the head counselor told me I had skipped a mandatory event—and I was fired for not attending. I had to clear out of the dorm. Later that day, I loaned my car to a guy, and he totaled it. In one day, I lost my job, my place to live, and my car. I was devastated.

"I told Coach Bowden what had happened, and he said, 'Meet me after practice, and we'll go over to the bank.' At the bank, Coach set up an account called Bobby Bowden Enterprises—a business name he came up with on the spot. He wrote me a check for a thousand dollars so I could get a place to stay. He wrote another check to cover my master's program tuition. He said I could eat my meals at the athletes' training table. Then he called the local Ford dealership and bought me a car. He paid me five hundred dollars a month as the only employee of Bobby Bowden Enterprises. And, of course, it all came out of Bobby's own pocket.

"I hadn't known the man more than a week, yet he sacrificed his own finances so I could stay. The 1974 season was a trying time for Coach Bowden. We ended with a 4–7 season and had a lot of problems with the team. The fans were angry, and they hung Coach Bowden in effigy from the trees on campus. Coach set an example of perseverance I'll never forget—and the next season, we had a terrific team and went to the Peach Bowl.

"After Coach Bowden left West Virginia, I began coaching at a high school in Blacksville, West Virginia. I was twenty-four years old. I've been coaching ever since—but I don't know how my life would have gone if not for Bobby Bowden's personal sacrifice for a grad assistant he didn't even know."

After interviewing scores of athletes who have played for Bobby, I keep hearing one theme repeated over and over again: Coach Bowden was a role model, and his players wanted to be like him.

Fullback Greg Jones, who plays for the Jacksonville Jaguars, told me, "As a young player, I began to think, 'When I get older I want to be like Coach Bowden and conduct my life just like he does.'" And strong safety Chris Hope, who now plays for the Tennessee Titans, told me, "Coach never told us to do something he wasn't already doing. Many leaders don't follow what they are saying. Coach always led by example." In *The Bowden Way: 50 Years of Leadership Wisdom*, Coach Bowden himself writes:

> If you wish to lead, you've got to lead by example, which means you've got to set the example. . . . *Don't do anything you don't mind everyone knowing about, because they eventually will know*. You're not one of the boys. You are their leader. You must act the part by adhering to a high moral standard.
>
> You are the standard-bearer for your organization. Whatever you expect from others, they'd better see it first in you. If you don't want this responsibility, then get out of the way and let someone else carry the flag. Your example will determine whether honesty is important on the job, whether loyalty will be shown to the organization, and whether people will work hard and have a good attitude, because they see how important those attributes are to you.[6]

To influence others, our actions and words must match. If you demand loyalty and integrity from your employees, you'd better be loyal and truthful toward them. If you preach Christian morality from the pulpit, there'd better not be any pornography on your hard drive. If you expect good sportsmanship from your players, you'd better watch your language the next time you shank it on the ninth hole.

In 2007, when Cal Ripken was inducted into the Baseball Hall of Fame, he gave a wise and insightful speech about influencing others through our actions. Here's a portion of that speech:

> As my major league career unfolded, I started paying a little more attention to my actions. I remember when Kenny Singleton showed me a tape of me throwing my helmet down after a strikeout and all he said was, "How does that look?" I remember learning about a family who saved their money to come to Baltimore to see me play. I got thrown out in the first inning and their little boy cried the whole game. . . .
>
> Kids see it all, and it's not just some of your actions that influence, it's all of them. Whether we like it or not as big leaguers, we are role models. The only question is will we be positive or will it be negative. . . .
>
> Sport can play a big role in teaching values and principles. It can be a huge developmental tool for life. Just think—teamwork, leadership, work ethic and trust are all part of the game, and are also factors in how we make the most of our lives. So an essential part of the job of every player . . . is to help the young people of today learn these lessons so they can live better lives tomorrow.[7]

That's the selfless attitude of Cal Ripken Jr. His influence on the fans—and especially his youngest fans—flows directly from his selflessness and willingness to serve his fans while asking nothing in return.

Baseball player and sportscaster Buddy Blattner recalls a story about longtime Red Sox outfielder Ted Williams. Along with fellow broadcaster Dizzy Dean, Blattner went to Boston to telecast several Red Sox games. They arrived at the Kenmore Hotel, where Ted Williams lived, and Ted came down to chat with his two old friends.

Buddy told Ted he had visited a hospital and met a ten-year-old boy who was a huge Ted Williams fan. The boy, who was dying of leukemia, received love and attention from the nurses. "Each day in the corridor," Blattner recalled, "they sat him on the floor with a little wooden bat and got on their hands and knees and rolled the ball to him. He'd hit it, and as it rolled they exclaimed, 'Oh, that's a double. That's a triple. That's a home run.' If it was a homer, it was hit by Ted!" The boy's hospital room was filled with Ted Williams memorabilia.

"When you see Ted," the youngster told Blattner, "tell him hello from me." When Buddy left the boy's room, the nurses stopped him in the hallway and asked if he could arrange for Ted Williams to send the boy a cap or autographed ball.

Williams (a WWII aviator who owned his own plane) said, "Bud, I'll tell you what—I'll fly in and see this boy—but on two conditions. . . . I want to be met at the airport by the boy's mother and father *only*. Any media or other gathering, and I'll just touch down and take right off again." Ted's second condition: Blattner could never report the incident on the air. Ted wanted a complete news blackout.

Blattner concluded that it was "one of the most heartwarming stories of my broadcasting career, and I couldn't tell it. The young boy died later in the year, but he enjoyed the greatest day of his life: a visit with his hero."[8] The great Ted Williams became even greater in my mind when I learned that he would go way out of his way to reach out to one sick boy and selflessly serve that boy, wanting nothing in return—not even some heartwarming publicity.

Let Them See Your Commitment

In 1978, maverick auto exec Lee Iacocca left Ford to become the head of the failing Chrysler Corporation. The following year, he convinced the U.S. government to guarantee $1.5 billion in loans to Chrysler, and within a few years, Iacocca succeeded in bringing the company back from the brink of calamity. He launched the first lines of minivans in America, repaid the government-backed loans seven years early, and retired in 1992 as one of the most celebrated business leaders in history.

In his autobiography, Iacocca says that one of his first challenges was to convince Chrysler workers and suppliers to make sacrificial concessions for the good of everyone. Without those concessions, Chrysler would fail and hundreds of thousands of people would lose their jobs. How did Iacocca persuade the workers and their union to make the necessary sacrifice? He did it by setting a *personal example* of sacrifice. Iacocca recalls:

> I began by reducing my own salary to $1.00 a year. Leadership means setting an example. When you find yourself in a position of leadership, people follow your every move. . . . When the leader talks, people listen. And when the leader acts, people watch. So you have to be careful about everything you say and everything you do.
>
> I didn't take $1.00 a year to be a martyr. I took it because I had to go into the pits. I took it so that when I went to Doug Fraser, the union president, I could look him in the eye and say: "Here's what I want from you guys as your share," and he couldn't come back to me and ask: ". . . What sacrifice have *you* made?" That's why I did it, for good, cold, pragmatic reasons. I wanted our employees and our suppliers to be thinking: "I can follow a guy who sets that kind of example."[9]

You can't influence others to make hard sacrifices while you dine on venison carpaccio with baby arugula. If you demand sacrifice from your family, your team, your employees, your soldiers, or your parishioners, you must set the example of sacrifice.

When we influence others by our actions, words are often unnecessary. General George Marshall (1880–1959) was chief of staff of the army during World War II. After the war, President Truman appointed him secretary of state. He formulated an ambitious program to rebuild war-ravaged Europe—the enormously effective Marshall Plan, for which he received the Nobel Peace Prize in 1953.

General Marshall believed in leading by influence, and influencing by example. In 1927, when he took command of the

Infantry School at Fort Benning, Georgia, he found the military post in a run-down state. The buildings needed paint and repair, and the grounds needed weeding and sprucing up. Instead of barking orders, General Marshall requisitioned paint supplies, building supplies, and gardening tools, then began fixing up his personal quarters.

The general never said a word to his subordinates—his actions spoke for him. He painted, cleaned, trimmed, mowed, and planted. When the other men on the base saw how General Marshall's quarters looked, they began cleaning and fixing up their billets as well. Within a few weeks, Fort Benning was transformed—by the quiet influence and example of General Marshall.[10]

One person's commitment to excellence can inspire others to pursue excellence as well. In 1998, rookie South Korean golfer Se Ri Pak won two major tournaments—the McDonald's LPGA Championship and the US Women's Open. At age twenty, and just two years after turning pro, Pak became the then-youngest winner of the US Women's Open. She also inspired a wave of "Seoul sisters"—young Korean golfers who experienced great success on women's golf tours around the world.

Prominent among the Seoul sisters is Inbee Park. She was only nine years old when her parents awakened her at 3:00 a.m. so that she could watch Se Ri Pak's superstar performance in the 1998 US Women's Open. Pak's thrilling win was a huge inspiration for young Park, who picked up a club for the first time just two days later.

On June 29, 2008, one decade after watching her idol win the US Women's Open, Inbee Park won the 2008 US Women's Open. It was her first LPGA tournament win. Park said, "I really would like to thank Se Ri for what she's done for Korean golf. Ten years ago, I was watching her winning this event on TV. I didn't know anything about golf back then. But it was very impressive for a little girl, just looking at her. I just thought that I could do it, too, so I just picked up a golf club."[11] Today, thousands of young girls are swinging clubs and dreaming of becoming the next Inbee Park, just as she dreamed of being the next Se Ri Pak.

Let them see your commitment to sacrifice, your commitment to hard work, and your commitment to excellence. Influence others by setting an example through your actions. Above all, influence others through your acts of grace, kindness, and forgiveness toward others.

In his autobiography, singer Tony Bennett (born Anthony Benedetto) recalls that his mother and father ran a neighborhood grocery store in New York City. The Benedetto family lived in an apartment over the store.

Once, during the depths of the Great Depression, a drunken man broke into the store at night, intending to rob the cash register. The robber made such a racket that Mr. Benedetto awoke and raced downstairs to investigate. He found the would-be robber sprawled across some crates, unconscious. Minutes later, the police arrived and roused the man. They told Mr. Benedetto that if he pressed charges, they'd haul the man to jail and lock him up.

Mr. Benedetto was a compassionate, forgiving man. He turned to the thief and said, "Do you have a job?"

"No."

"Well, you have one now if you want it. How would you like to work for me?"

Mr. Benedetto gave the man a job on the spot.

"You can't beat that kind of thoughtfulness," Tony Bennett concluded. "It wasn't charity; it was an example of the kind of human spirit that kept people going. After all, we were all in the same boat."[12]

Mr. Benedetto graciously forgave a man who tried to steal from him. Whenever we forgive and restore people who have done wrong to us, we impact lives in a powerful way. That's influence in action.

Let Your Actions Speak

I am very impressed by the influence of Donovan McNabb, who was always mindful of the impact of his actions on the people around him. Donovan was the Philadelphia Eagles' quarterback from 1999 to 2009, and also played for the Redskins and the Vikings. He led the Eagles to five NFC championship games and one Super Bowl. After his rookie year with the Eagles, he started the Donovan McNabb Foundation to fund diabetes research. Both his father and brother are diabetic, and Donovan has sponsored many children to attend American Diabetes Association youth camps, where he often conducts football clinics for campers.[13]

I was honored when Donovan invited me to give the keynote address at his foundation's inaugural dinner at Chicago's Hyatt Regency Hotel in June 2000. I sat at the table with Donovan, his fiancée (now wife), Raquel, his parents, Sam and Wilma, and his brother, Sean. It was obvious to me that the McNabbs were a unique family, close-knit and dedicated to Christian values. During the evening, it was clear that Sam and Wilma McNabb raised their two sons to use their influence wisely.

"My parents raised me to set a good example," he told me, "and to never let success go to my head. They told me that people are watching, whether I know it or not, so I had to be a good role model, first, last, and always."

Donovan's father Sam once told the *Washington Post*, "I taught both my children, 'Let your actions speak.' There's a strong scripture in Proverbs that says if you train a child in the proper direction, when he grows older he will not depart. . . . [Donovan has] handled some situations better than I would have. I'm proud to see his growth and development as a man. I'm proud he lets his actions represent him."[14]

Donovan McNabb has weathered storms of adversity and opposition, yet you never hear him argue with his critics or defend himself. He lets his actions speak for him. In game eleven of the 2002 season, he was sacked early in the first quarter by Arizona Cardinals safety Adrian Wilson. The team doctor examined his ankle in the locker room and decided that Donovan had a bad sprain. Donovan told the doctor to tape up the ankle and let him back in the game. Though the pain was excruciating, Donovan played the rest of the game, completing 20 of 25 for 255 yards and four touchdowns—and the Eagles won, 38–14. Only after the game did x-rays reveal that instead of a sprained ankle, he had a fibula that was broken in three places. It takes some kind of toughness to play three and a half quarters of pro football on a broken calf bone.

In September of the following year, Donovan McNabb was the object of a controversial statement by radio host Rush Limbaugh, who was then an ESPN commentator. Mixing social commentary with football analysis, Limbaugh opined, "I think what we've had here is a little social concern in the NFL. The media has been very desirous that a black quarterback do well. . . . McNabb got a lot of the credit for the performance of the team that he really didn't deserve."[15]

Limbaugh's comments didn't fit the facts. Though the Eagles had gotten off to a slow start for the 2003 season, McNabb proved Limbaugh wrong by amassing the second-best QB rating in the NFL for the second half of the season while leading the Eagles to the NFC Championship game. It can be argued that McNabb's on-field stats were hurt by one of the least productive squads of wide receivers in the NFL. The following season, with the addition of superstar receiver Terrell Owens, McNabb led the Eagles all the way to the Super Bowl XXXIX. Though the Eagles lost to the New England Patriots, Donovan McNabb answered Limbaugh's words with action.

Another unfair charge often leveled at black athletes of good moral character is that they "aren't black enough." Donovan McNabb has drawn this sort of attack from several critics, notably boxer Bernard "The Executioner" Hopkins. In a May 2011 article, *Philadelphia Daily News* writer Marcus Hayes wrote, "According to Hopkins, McNabb had a privileged childhood in suburban Chicago and, as a result, is not black enough or tough enough."[16]

What "privileged childhood" is Hopkins talking about? The McNabb family lived on the notoriously crime-ridden South Side of Chicago. Sam worked as an electrical engineer and Wilma worked as a nurse. They scrimped and saved, and were eventually able to move out of the South Side to Dolton, an all-white Chicago suburb. The McNabbs were middle-class, not "privileged"—and being the first black family in the neighborhood resulted in some shattered windows and obscene graffiti on the walls of their home. (Is that "black enough" for you, Mr. Hopkins?)

Whether in Chicago's South Side facing street crime or in the suburbs facing white prejudice, the McNabb family showed great courage. Sam and Wilma consistently taught their sons Sean and Donovan the value of faith, hard work, courage, and character. They taught their sons to take a quiet stand for what's right, to ignore the yammering of their critics—and to let their actions speak.

That's how Donovan McNabb plays his game, leads his life, and impacts the world with his influence. As his father Sam once said, "Words don't always communicate effectively. Actions take care of any uncertainty."[17]

As I was putting the finishing touches on this book, I heard the news that songwriter Robert Sherman had died in London. I interviewed Robert Sherman and his brother Richard a few years ago. The Sherman brothers composed songs and film scores for *The Parent Trap*, *Mary Poppins*, *The Jungle Book*, and the song for the Disney theme park attraction "It's a Small World." The news of Robert Sherman's passing reminded me of a phone conversation I had with his brother Richard about a song they had written for *Mary Poppins*.

During the last two years of Walt Disney's life, the Sherman brothers would stop by Walt's office every Friday at closing time. "We had our own little private ceremony," Richard told me. "Walt would ask us what we were working on, and we'd tell him. Then he'd say, 'Play the song, Richard.' I knew which song he meant. I'd play 'Feed the Birds' from *Mary Poppins*. Walt had a piano in his office; I'd play the song while Walt looked out the north window of his office. When the song was over, he'd say, 'Yep, that's what it is all about. Have a good weekend, boys.' And with that, he'd send us home.

"'Feed the Birds' is a song about the old woman who sells bread crumbs in front of St. Paul's Cathedral. She says, 'Feed the birds, tuppence a bag.' And, of course, the song is not really about feeding the birds. It's about showing kindness to other people. It doesn't cost much to be kind to one another, just 'tuppence,' a couple of pennies, practically nothing at all.

"Walt understood what Bob and I were saying through that song. I think that's why it became his favorite song. It was the first song we wrote for the picture—our first inspiration after we read 'The Bird Woman' chapter in P. L. Travers' original book. It was the song we played for Walt at our first story meeting, and the last thing we played for him. When we wrote it, we knew it was the metaphor for the whole picture.

"Even after Walt passed away in 1966, I continued going to his office on Friday afternoons, and I'd play the song for him. It was a very personal thing for me.

"On Walt's hundredth birthday, they had a big celebration in the middle of Disneyland. They had a piano and they asked me to sing 'Feed the Birds.' I sang it, and I choked up, but I got through it. As I was singing, a beautiful gray dove flew right by me and then up again into the sky. Don't tell me there is no God in the heavens!"

As Richard told me this story, he choked up—and so did I. After a few moments, I said, "Richard, could I ask a favor? Could we sing that song together?" He agreed, so over the phone, without accompaniment, we began to sing "Feed the Birds" together. We didn't get far before we both choked with emotion.

It was a moment I'll never forget—the moment I sang a few bars of that beautiful song with the man who wrote it. It's a song about influencing others with our acts of kindness. It doesn't cost much to touch another soul.

Questions for Group Discussion or Individual Reflection

Chapter 5: The Influence of Our Actions

1. When it comes to your influence on others, what carries more weight—actions or words? Explain your answer and give examples from your own experience.

2. Was there ever a time in your life when you were profoundly impacted by a person's actions alone? Describe what happened and how that incident influenced your life. Does that event still guide and shape the person you are today?

3. Consider the story of Ted Williams visiting the young fan who had leukemia. Why do you think Ted Williams was so adamant that there be no media coverage of his meeting with the boy? If you had been in his position, would you have set the same conditions?

4. Is there a situation in your life where you would like to have some influence, but you know your words are not welcome? For example, you'd like to reach out to someone who is hurting, but he or she is not receptive to other people right now. Can you think of some way you might be able to influence that person through actions alone? What are some actions you might take?

5. The author quotes Jack E. Shaw who wrote, "We are God's ambassadors—God's hands extended to others." An ambassador is a representative who is empowered to speak on behalf of someone else. If we are God's ambassadors, we represent God and we speak for Him. How does it affect the way you see yourself to know that you are "God's ambassador"? Think back over the past week; do you think you have been a good ambassador and that you have represented God well? Do your actions reflect well on God? Why or why not? What steps can you take this coming week to be a better ambassador for Him?

6. Donovan McNabb's father, Sam McNabb, said, "Words don't always communicate effectively. Actions take care of any uncertainty." What steps can you take this week to ensure that your actions communicate effectively, and in a way that is consistent with your words? Give specific examples. Commit yourself to making those specific changes in your actions and behavior this week.

6

The Influence of Our Words

Scientific men tell us that every sound upon the
surface of our own and other planets circulates in
endless and ceaseless waves through infinite space.
Certainly not less subtle is the influence of our words
upon the life and character of the world.

Augustus Woodbury, *Plain Words
to Young Men*, 1858[1]

In the 1970s, when I was living in Philadelphia, I became acquainted with a fascinating and immensely influential man
named Arthur S. DeMoss. We became good friends and he
shared his story with me. Art DeMoss came from a rough-and-
tumble background, making his living on the wrong side of the
law. He was a successful bookie in his early twenties, running
a couple of highly profitable horse-betting rooms in Albany,
New York. He made so much money that, as a young man of
twenty-four, he owned three brand-new Cadillacs.

At age twenty-five, Art attended a tent-revival meeting and
experienced a life-changing encounter with Jesus Christ. He left

113

the rackets, and founded a life insurance company that eventually became a financial empire. He used the proceeds of that empire to expand his influence and help spread the Christian message that had so completely changed his life.

Art DeMoss was a rough-around-the-edges, plainspoken man, with as big a heart as anyone I've ever known. One of the ways he used his influence was to host outreach dinners. He would invite some of the most accomplished and influential people in the country to his home. There were often as many as two hundred people in attendance—which gives you some sense of how big his house was. Art would usually invite a guest speaker, and then he would get up and tell his own story. Though Art was not a polished speaker, people responded to his life story and his humble spirit.

Art also hosted Bible studies in his home, with about fifteen to twenty people attending. One night, he said, "I want to hear everyone's testimony. Let's go around the room and each one of us can tell how we met Jesus Christ." So, one by one, each person told the story of his or her encounter with Christ—until we got to a young man named Doug. When it was his turn to speak, Doug said, "I don't have a testimony."

"Come with me," Art said. He led Doug into the next room. About twenty minutes later, Art and Doug returned to the group.

"Doug will now share his testimony," Art said. And Doug told us how Art DeMoss had just led him to faith in Jesus Christ.

On September 1, 1979, Art was on the tennis court. He tossed the ball in the air to serve it—and suffered a massive heart attack. Doctors later said he was dead before the ball bounced once. He was only fifty-three years old.

I got the news that same day, and I rushed to the DeMoss home. I was met at the door by one of Art's daughters, who was in her late teens. "How is your family doing?" I asked.

"We're pretty rejoicing," she said, though her smile was sad. I knew exactly what "pretty rejoicing" meant. The loss is painful—but when you know you'll see your loved one again in eternity, you can rejoice even in the loss.

Art's close friend, Bill Bright, the founder of Campus Crusade for Christ, officiated at the funeral. Bill looked out across a sea of mourners and asked, "Would everyone who is going to heaven because of Arthur DeMoss please raise your hand?"

I saw hundreds of hands go up all around me. I thought, *Wow! What an influence Art had. What a legacy he left.* Arthur DeMoss never hesitated to speak up and say what needed to be said. He was never shy about telling his story and spreading his influence with his words.

Influence Is a Two-Way Street

In 1994, Duke forward Grant Hill was selected by the Detroit Pistons in the NBA draft. He came into the league with high expectations, and was hailed by many as "the next Michael Jordan."

The Pistons came to Orlando early in the season, and I went to the locker room, eager to meet this young man whose college career I had followed closely (Grant had played for Coach Mike Krzyzewski at Duke). When the Pistons came out for their pre-game warm-up, I approached him and said, "Grant, I just want you to know—I believe you can have an enormous influence in this league, on and off the court. You can make a huge difference because of who you are." He shook my hand and thanked me, then went out onto the court. Our entire conversation lasted thirty seconds at most.

Fast-forward to the year 2000. That's the year the Orlando Magic acquired Grant Hill as a free agent. Soon after Grant's arrival in Orlando, he came to me and said, "I will never forget that little chat you had with me before my first game here in Orlando. I've always tried to remember those words and live up to them. I've always set a goal of having a positive influence in this league."

When Grant Hill reminded me of that conversation, I felt a tingle up my spine. It had been six years, and I probably would have forgotten that conversation if Grant hadn't reminded me. That incident spoke to me of how important it is to remind young people of the influence they have, and of how important it is for them to use their influence wisely.

What we say sticks. Our words have a greater influence than we can ever know.

I saw Grant use his own influence in a positive way during his seven years in Orlando. He was hindered by ankle injuries soon after his arrival, and in 2003, he underwent a major operation to refracture and realign his ankle. After that surgery, he developed a methicillin-resistant *Staphylococcus aureus* (MRSA) infection—an extremely serious infection that is sometimes fatal. He received intravenous antibiotics for the next six months.

Grant came roaring back for us in the 2004–05 season, but struggled with injuries again the following season. Through all of the adversity he battled, Grant Hill maintained his character and his influence. As Brandon Land of *Bleacher Report* observed, "Grant Hill is the perfect example of an athlete who feels the responsibility to be a role model. Throughout his career, Hill has willingly taken on the pressure of having people look up to him. Not only has he shown a humility rarely seen in a modern professional athlete, his perseverance through the toughest times makes him a guy you just can't help but like."[2]

Always conscious of the impact and influence of his own words, he very graciously reminded me of the influence of my words to him. That's one of the powerful dimensions of this thing called influence: Words of influence flow both ways. You influence me with your words, and I, in turn, influence you with mine.

While I was working on this book, I received a handwritten note in the mail that absolutely knocked my socks off:

Pat—
I just listened to you on the radio. I didn't realize that you were battling cancer. Your attitude is unbelievable, as

always. That will be the number one thing that will put you ahead of that disease.

My mother, Dr. E. E. Leon, spent her whole professional life working to cure breast cancer. She would tell me that a positive attitude and an attack mode to win are primary to a successful cure rate.

Thank you again for the books you write. I have an English degree that has been put on the shelf, so I appreciate your talents. You are a great example to all of us in so many ways. The Magic are lucky to have you.

> *Sincerely, your friend,*
> *Andy Reid*
> *Head Coach,*
> *The Philadelphia Eagles*

What a humbling and moving experience it is to know that something I said on the radio has influenced Andy Reid. And what a healing experience it is for me to receive his words of encouragement and influence for my life. Influence is a two-way street, and one of the greatest ways we can influence each other is by encouraging, inspiring, and motivating each other by what we say.

The Life-Changing Power of Our Words

One person can change the course of another person's life with the power of words alone.

Track and field athlete Florence Griffith-Joyner was affectionately known to millions as "Flo-Jo" and "The Fastest Woman of All Time." In 1988, she achieved world records in the 100 and 200 meter events—records that stand to this day. In September 1998, the world was stunned to learn that Flo-Jo had passed away due to a massive epileptic seizure that stopped her breathing while she slept. She was thirty-eight years old.

I met Flo-Jo in 1995. She and I were seated next to each other at a dinner, and she told me her story of growing up poor in

South Central Los Angeles. Her eyes lit up when she told me about meeting boxing champ Sugar Ray Robinson when she was just eight years old.

"Sugar Ray looked me in the eye," she said, "and he told me, 'It doesn't matter where you come from, what your color is, or what the odds are against you. All that matters is that you have a dream, and you commit yourself to that dream. Do that, and it *will* happen.' Right then and there, I was sold. I was just eight years old, but I was all fired up about what my future could be."

With words alone, Sugar Ray Robinson changed the course of one girl's life. Flo-Jo's time on earth was all too short, but she reached a level of achievement that has never been matched because Sugar Ray gave her the power to believe she could do it. What words of influence do you have for the young people around you?

My cancer diagnosis has sensitized me to the power of words to influence others. These days, I pay more attention than ever before to the phone calls, letters, and emails I receive. I'm aware that some little paragraph I write back or some remark I make in a media interview could have a huge impact on someone's life. Lately, I invest more thought and prayer in every word I write and speak.

Some years ago, I was having lunch with my sister. She was in her early sixties and we were reminiscing about our years growing up together in Wilmington, Delaware. At one point, she got a wistful look in her eyes and said, "Growing up, nobody ever told me I looked nice. Mom and dad, my siblings, my friends, even my boyfriends—nobody ever said to me, 'Ruth, you look nice. You look pretty in that dress. I like the way you did your hair.' The first person to ever tell me I looked nice was the man I married."

Ooh, that hit me hard. I thought, *Shame on you, Pat Williams. What a missed opportunity.* I'm Ruth's older brother, and she looked to me for affirmation. Why didn't I ever think to give her the few positive words that would have meant so much to her? Why couldn't I have just said, "Ruth, you look really nice tonight"?

That conversation was a wake-up call. Now, with my children and grandchildren, and especially with the girls, I try to give that affirmation—not empty or false praise, but a well-chosen compliment when they have gone out of their way to dress up and do their hair and makeup just right. I know now how much an affirming word can mean to a girl.

It just takes a little thoughtfulness to make a difference in the lives of other people. I'm reminded of an incident in *A Model for a Better Future* by supermodel Kim Alexis. She was having dinner at a Florida restaurant with wealthy, powerful friends. As the waiter refilled her water glass, Kim said, "Thank you."

The man across the table said, "You don't have to thank those people! You're better than they are."

Kim was shocked—she had never considered herself better than anyone. "That waiter," she replied, "is just as important as I am. It's just common courtesy to say thank you when someone does something nice for you."

The man looked at her aghast. "Really, Kim! That guy gets paid minimum wage to fill people's water glasses! You're on the cover of *Vogue* and *Sports Illustrated*! You've done so much more than people like that! Of course, you're better than they are! You should realize who you are!"

Kim Alexis concluded, "That conversation was a real eye-opener to me. Since then, I've encountered many people who consider themselves better than others—and I find that completely baffling. Aren't we all God's children? Aren't we all equal in His sight?"[3]

She's right. We are all equal in God's sight—and we owe each other the simple gift of kind words and common courtesy. As columnist Dave Barry once observed, "A person who is nice to you, but rude to the waiter, is not a nice person."[4] Treating other people with respect, kindness, and dignity is a simple yet powerful way of using our words as an influence for good.

Slender Threads and Pixie Dust

For more than three decades, Fred Rogers of *Mister Rogers' Neighborhood* was a soft-spoken role model of compassion, tolerance, and good moral values. He has received every honor a grateful society can bestow, from the Presidential Medal of Freedom and a Peabody Award to an asteroid named in his honor—26858 Misterrogers, somewhere between the orbits of Mars and Jupiter. *Esquire* writer Tom Junod recalled what Mister Rogers told the audience when he received the Lifetime Achievement Award at the 1997 Daytime Emmys:

> He made his small bow and said into the microphone, "All of us have special ones who have loved us into being. Would you just take, along with me, ten seconds to think of the people who have helped you become who you are . . . Ten seconds of silence." And then he lifted his wrist, and looked at the audience, and looked at his watch, and said softly, "I'll watch the time," and there was, at first, a small whoop from the crowd, a giddy, strangled hiccup of laughter, as people realized that he wasn't kidding. . . . One second, two seconds, three seconds . . . and now the jaws clenched, and the bosoms heaved, and the mascara ran, and the tears fell upon the beglittered gathering like rain leaking down a crystal chandelier, and Mister Rogers finally looked up from his watch and said, "May God be with you" to all his vanquished children.[5]

In his gentle, quiet way, Mister Rogers was an authority figure. He was the farthest thing imaginable from an authoritarian— but he spoke with a sweet, genuine, and irresistible authority that comes from a love of humanity, and especially a love of children. When he told his audience to take ten seconds to think of the people who had influenced them and shaped their lives, the people in the audience obeyed.

In *The World According to Mister Rogers*, Fred Rogers tells the story of going to the White House to give a speech about children and television. Just as he had at the Emmy Awards event, he asked the audience to pause in silence and think of someone in their lives who had helped shape them into the people they had become. Then he recalled what happened after he gave his speech:

> As I was leaving that enormous room, I heard something from one of the military guards who was all dressed up in white and gold, looking like a statue. I heard him whisper, "Thanks, Mister Rogers."
>
> So I went over to him and noticed his eyes were moist and he said, "Well, sir, as I listened to you today, I started to remember my grandfather's brother. I haven't thought about him in years. I was only seven when he died, but just before that, he gave me his favorite fishing rod. I've just been thinking, maybe that's why I like fishing so much and why I like to show the kids in my neighborhood all about it."
>
> Well, as far as I'm concerned, the major reason for my going to Washington that day was that military guard and nourishing the memory of his great-uncle. What marvelous mysteries we're privileged to be part of! Why would that young man be assigned to guard that particular room on that particular day? Slender threads like that weave this complex fabric of our life together.[6]

Slender threads indeed—threads of influence, woven into complex patterns by our words. Don't you want to have that kind of influence on people wherever you go? Don't you want to be able to stir up memories and warm thoughts and feelings wherever you go? I know I do. I want to have that kind of influence on the people around me. I want my words to have that kind of impact.

I'm reminded of the Old Testament prophet Samuel. The Bible tells us, "The Lord was with Samuel as he grew up, and he let none of Samuel's words fall to the ground" (1 Samuel 3:19). Every word of Samuel was a word of power and influence. God didn't let a single word from his lips fall to the ground and be wasted. For the rest of my life, I want the same thing to be said of me—that God let none of my words fall to the ground.

Ana Dutra is CEO of Korn/Ferry Leadership and Talent Consulting. Born in Ipanema, Brazil, she earned degrees in economics and law at two different schools in Rio de Janeiro— simultaneously. While working as a lawyer and studying for her master's, she was recruited by IBM, and came to America in 1992. In an article for the *New York Times*, she recalled some of the best advice she ever received:

> I have never forgotten something that a boss told me early in my consulting career. He asked me what we did for clients, and I said we helped them achieve their highest performance level. He said, "No, what do you really do?" And I said, "We advise clients on their growth strategies." He said that I didn't get it, and that we really gave clients "pixie dust." He explained that all executives have ambition, but that they don't believe they can fly. We were there to sprinkle pixie dust, the way Tinker Bell did in *Peter Pan*, and to hold their hand so they could achieve things they never thought possible. It taught me empathy. Sometimes, I bring glitter to meetings to make his point.[7]

That's how you and I need to see the words we speak. Our words are like pixie dust that we sprinkle all around us. Our job as people of influence is to convince others that they can fly. When they *believe* they can fly, they usually *do*.

A Foundation of Truth

One of the best ways to use our words to influence others is to simply *tell the truth*. All too often, people try to influence others with manipulation, deception, false flattery, ingratiation, covering up, making excuses, spin doctoring, little white lies, and great big whopping lies. We may get by for a while by playing fast and loose with the truth, but over time, honesty is still the best policy. If we want to influence others in a positive way, we have to tell the truth.

Former NFL coach Mike Holmgren has built a reputation for total candor and truthfulness. He has often said, "If you ask me a question, make sure you want to know the answer." And sports agent Bob LaMonte says of Holmgren, "I've never known him to tell a lie. . . . Players respect him because he will tell the truth." In *Winning the NFL Way*, LaMonte tells about a free agent wide receiver Coach Holmgren wanted to recruit to the Seattle Seahawks roster. The player was distrustful because he had been lied to before, and he wanted to be sure that Holmgren was leveling with him.

"Look," Holmgren said, "we want you here. We have a role for you on our team, but you're not going to be a starter. We have two young players that we plan on giving every opportunity to be the starters. Now if one of them gets hurt, or he can't do it, then yes, absolutely, you'll get an opportunity to start. But I'm not going to tell you what you want to hear so you'll sign."

That was all the player needed to know. He knew he could trust an honest caveat more than a glib assurance. He respected Coach Holmgren's candor and signed on for a year. During that year, Holmgren often made him a starter in games with three-wide-receiver formations. After the first year, the player continued signing on for additional seasons and had a great career with the Seahawks. That never would have happened if he suspected Holmgren of leading him on.

Coach Holmgren later said, "My philosophy is that honesty has to permeate your entire existence. You must live your life this way, at the office and away from the office. This is where you start, because if you lose trust, you can't teach. You can't communicate. Your people won't listen to you and you'll never be able to get them to do what needs to be done."[8] In short, dishonesty kills influence; the impact of influence is built on a foundation of ethical behavior and truth.

Pastor, level with your congregation. Coach, level with your players. Military leader, level with your troops. Business leader, level with your subordinates. The truth builds trust, and trust generates influence.

When Herb Kelleher was the CEO of Southwest Airlines, he leveled with his people in both good times and bad. Once, when he learned that Southwest was heading toward an unprofitable quarter, he issued a memo to all of his people, from the pilots to the desk agents to the maintenance crew, explaining the company's fiscal problems. Then he asked everyone in the Southwest family to pull together and urged each employee to save just five dollars of company money per day. As a result of Herb Kelleher's candid memo, Southwest Airlines trimmed 5.6 percent from its operating expenses that quarter—and the company ended the quarter in the black.[9] The moral to the story: Honesty really is the best policy—and the key to influence.

We also expand our influence by speaking the truth about our own failures and frailties, and by letting others see that we struggle just as they do. In this book and in all my other books, I have tried to be truthful about my failures and struggles. I've talked about my spiritual failings, my character flaws, my immaturity in my early years, and the mistakes I've made as a leader. Most recently, I've written honestly about the battle I'm now waging against cancer. Again and again, the letters, emails, and phone calls I receive confirm that people gain the most help and encouragement when I am transparent and candid about the struggles in my life.

Betty Ford was first lady of the United States from 1974 to 1977, while Gerald Ford was president. She was a forthright lady who never shied away from speaking the truth as she saw it. When she was diagnosed with breast cancer and underwent a mastectomy in 1974, she spoke candidly about her experience and began a national discussion about breast cancer that undoubtedly saved thousands of lives. She didn't hold back on any hot-button issue, but spoke her mind on feminism, the Equal Rights Amendment, sex, and morality. She not only spoke openly and unabashedly about her years-long struggle with alcoholism in the 1970s, but she founded the Betty Ford Center for substance abuse and addiction in Rancho Mirage, California.

Because she was willing to speak the truth about her own life, including her struggles and imperfections, she had an influence that some say far outshone the influence of her husband, the president of the United States. The *New York Times* once observed, "Mrs. Ford's impact on American culture may be far wider and more lasting than that of her husband, who served a mere 896 days, much of it spent trying to restore the dignity of the office of the president."[10]

After Betty Ford died at the age of ninety-three, her successor as first lady, Rosalynn Carter, recalled her fondly in a piece for *Time* magazine. Mrs. Carter wrote:

> Her openness and candor about her struggles with substance abuse and cancer made her human. Everybody loved her.
>
> I was with Betty the first time she spoke out about her addiction. It was at a press conference. . . . Someone asked if she was on something, and she said, "Yes, I take Valium every day." You could see the pencils come out of the reporters' pockets. I thought it was interesting that she would say this, but I don't think either one of us realized what a stir she had created.
>
> Betty Ford was a role model to me. . . . There is no way to know how many lives she touched and made better because of her willingness to speak out.[11]

Mrs. Carter is talking about Betty Ford's influence—the kind of influence that can only come about as the result of honest, candid talk. There is no more dependable foundation for a lifetime of influence than a foundation of truth.

Words That Build, Words That Tear Down

As this book was nearing completion, Orlando hosted the NBA All-Star Weekend. One of the annual events in the All-Star Weekend is the Legends Brunch on Sunday, put on by the Retired Players Association. I was one of several individuals honored at the brunch, and civil rights leader Jesse Jackson also attended. I've known Jesse for many years, going back to when I was general manager of the Chicago Bulls and he was a regular attendee at our games. During the brunch, Jesse sought me out and said, "What's going on with Dwight Howard?"

At that time, our star center, Dwight Howard, was talking openly about the possibility of being traded to another team. He would not commit to staying in Orlando, but said instead that he wanted to explore all of his options and give the Magic an opportunity to trade him. This had been going on for months.

So Jesse asked me, "What's going on with Dwight Howard? What's the young man thinking about? He could own this town. He *should* own this town. He should have a hotel named after him out on the hotel strip. He has no business leaving Orlando. I don't usually give out my phone number, but please give Dwight my number. Have him call me. I think I could have a real positive influence on him."

So Jesse gave me his phone number, and I passed it on to Dwight. I know that Dwight and Jesse talked, and though I don't know what these gentlemen said to each other, I do know that, less than three weeks later, Dwight Howard agreed to play at least one more season in Orlando. Was Jesse's influence a factor in Dwight's decision? I'll let you be the judge of that.

I once heard retired Dodgers manager Tommy Lasorda speak about a time that he and Ted Williams were hanging out after an awards dinner on the East Coast. They went up to Tommy's hotel room and talked until 3:00 a.m. Finally, Ted said to Tommy, "You know Frank Sinatra, don't you?"

"Sure," Tommy said. "He's a good friend."

"Well, Tommy, next time you see him, tell him how much I like his music."

"Why don't you tell him yourself? I'll call him right now."

It was three a.m. their time, but only midnight in Palm Springs, and Tommy knew that Frank would be up. So Tommy dialed Frank's number and said, "Hey, Frankie, there's a guy here who wants to talk to you." Then he put Ted Williams on the phone.

For the next ten minutes, Ted talked to Frank Sinatra about music, and Frank talked to Ted Williams about baseball. Finally, Ted handed the phone back to Tommy. "Can you believe it?" he said. "I was just talking to Frank Sinatra—and he's a fan!"

At the same time, Tommy heard Frank Sinatra's voice from the phone, saying, "Tommy, can you believe it? I just talked to Ted Williams, and he likes my music! Isn't that amazing? Ted Williams!"

That's how you and I should use our words—to build other people up, to encourage and empower, to affirm and bless. Positive words produce positive influence.

In 1999, CBS News interviewed Ron Prescott Reagan, the youngest of President Reagan's four children. Correspondent Leslie Stahl asked Ron Reagan to describe his famous father. "I have never seen him belittle anyone," the younger Reagan said. "I have never heard him gossip about anyone. . . . He's a nice man to the core and a terribly dignified man. . . . All his children loved him desperately. . . . When you're faced with an ethical decision, perhaps, a decision of right or wrong, you could do worse than ask yourself what he might do."[12]

Can the same be said of you and me? Can it be said that we have never belittled anyone, gossiped about anyone, that we are "nice to the core" and role models of ethical decision making? Don't you want that kind of reputation? I know I do. As people of influence, we set the tone for the people around us. If we set an example of only spreading "good gossip," of only speaking well of others, of only building others up, then we will have a healthy and far-reaching influence. If we spread malicious gossip, we are poisoning our own well and destroying our influence with others.

One of the wisest, most influential people who ever lived— King Solomon of ancient Israel—once warned, "When a leader listens to malicious gossip, all the workers get infected with evil" (Proverbs 29:12, THE MESSAGE). So never miss the opportunity to say a kind or encouraging word. If you speak only good things about other people, you will never need to whisper.

One of the most destructive things we can do with our words is to gossip. Simply defined, gossip is spreading information about the personal matters of other people. King Solomon put it this way:

> A scoundrel plots evil,
>> and on their lips it is like a scorching fire.
> A perverse person stirs up conflict,
>> and a gossip separates close friends.
>>> Proverbs 16:27–28

Some people will say, "But this isn't gossip—it's all true." But it really doesn't matter if the information you spread is "true" or not. If it's none of your business and if it's none of the business of the person you're telling, then "true" or not, it's gossip—and it's destructive.

And let's not kid ourselves—most of the information we think is "true" is actually slanted, incomplete, unreliable, and unverified. The main thing we are interested in is not whether its "true," but whether it's "juicy." Before you spread information about another person, you might ask yourself these seven questions:

1. Am I going to harm someone's reputation?
2. Am I willing to go straight to that person and discuss the matter privately?
3. Is the person I'm telling in a position to deal with the matter?
4. Am I betraying someone's trust? If so, do I have a good reason for doing so? (For example, if someone informs you that he's planning murder or suicide, you should report that to someone who can intervene.)
5. Am I willing to be identified as the source of the story?
6. Are my motives pure—and am I seeking attention or trying to hurt someone?
7. Am I obeying the Golden Rule? How would I feel if someone spread this story about me?

Gossip destroys families, churches, teams, and organizations. It erodes morale and disrupts relationships, resulting in a loss of unity and productivity. If you develop a reputation as a gossip, it will damage your influence. People will learn that you can't be trusted, and that you are willing to hurt others with your words.

If you want to spread positive rumors that build people up and enhance their reputations, feel free! Spread as much *good* news about people as you like.

Wise old King Solomon also urged us to use the influence of our words to bring peace out of conflict. He wrote:

> A gentle answer turns away wrath,
>   but a harsh word stirs up anger.
> The tongue of the wise adorns knowledge,
>   but the mouth of the fool gushes folly.
>   Proverbs 15:1–2

In April 1967, I had an experience that vividly illustrated Solomon's advice. I was the general manager of the Spartanburg Phillies. The Phillies front office sent Bobby Malkmus, a former big league infielder, to Spartanburg to help coach some of our rookie ballplayers for a few weeks. I was excited to have Bobby joining our operation in Spartanburg, because I knew his major league reputation would draw bigger crowds to our games.

Bobby Malkmus was a man of strong Christian convictions. He didn't drink, cuss, or chew tobacco. But Bobby was far more impressive because of the things he *did* do than the things he *didn't*. Bobby was an openhearted, likable guy who made friends wherever he went. He knew more about the game of baseball than anyone I had ever met. And he had some of the best people skills I've ever seen in action. Above all, Bobby Malkmus possessed a Solomon-like wisdom for finding a fair solution to any problem. He always knew exactly what to say and how to say it.

One early Saturday morning, my phone rang. It was the Spartanburg police, and the officer told me that three of our ballplayers had brawled in a beer joint, putting one customer in the hospital. The players had then boarded the team bus and left on a road trip. After talking to the officer, I sighed and called the office in Philly. The Philadelphia office called our team manager at the team's next stop and ordered him to send the three offending players back to Spartanburg for disciplinary action.

My job was to impose the penalty: Two players would be summarily released, while the third would be fined and suspended. All three were scheduled to arrive by taxicab on Sunday evening.

I was scared to death. How do you give that kind of news to three guys who had already beaten up a guy in a bar? I'd be facing a three-man wrecking crew all alone, and they had very little to lose by working me over. I needed some backup. So I called Bobby Malkmus and we had breakfast at a diner while I filled him in on the situation.

"Tell you what," Bobby said at last. "Let's go to the ballpark together and meet those guys. If there are two of us, there shouldn't be any trouble." I was so relieved to hear that, I could have hugged Bobby!

We went to the ballpark and waited. Finally, the taxi pulled up and the three players got out. I thought they'd be spoiling for a fight. Instead, they looked defeated and scared. As it turned out, I didn't need Bobby for protection. Instead, I needed Bobby's wisdom and compassion. I was at a loss for words—but Bobby knew *exactly* what to say.

Bobby wrapped his arms around the shoulders of the two men who were cut from the team. "I'm so sorry, fellas," he said. "I feel sick having to tell you this, but the front office says we have to release you. If there's anything I can do, just name it."

Of course, there wasn't anything Bobby could do. There wasn't anything I could do. But Bobby knew exactly what to say. He didn't suggest that the Phillies organization was unfair or that the punishment was too harsh. He just spoke as a compassionate friend.

I was amazed to see how Bobby used his words of wisdom to defuse a potentially explosive situation. And it was a lesson to me in how to handle a crisis. Bobby Malkmus did more than bring peace out of conflict. He influenced those three young men with the gracious impact of his words—and he also had a huge influence on a wet-behind-the-ears minor league general manager named Pat Williams.

Years later, I learned that when it comes to words of influence, what goes around comes around. I was sitting in a conference room at the Orlando Magic facility. There were about twenty or so Magic executives in that room, being taught by Al Lucia, a highly regarded speaker, trainer, and human resources consultant. During his presentation, he used a projector to flash quotations and bullet points on the screen behind him. At one point, he flashed this quote on the screen:

I'll show you some of the amazing wonders that have come about because people dared to dream their dreams—and then had the courage, ingenuity, and perseverance to hammer those dreams into reality!

I read those words and thought, *Wow, I like that quote! I've got to write that down!* So I opened my notebook and began scribbling those words as fast as I could write. Then Al put the name of the author of that quote on the screen:

Pat Williams,
in *Go for the Magic*

The room exploded in laughter. Everyone had seen me furiously writing down my own quotation! It just goes to show: When you send out your words of influence, you never know when they might come back to you.

So as you send your words of impact and influence out into the world, remember that words spoken in a whisper often return like thunder. Make sure the words you speak are words you'll be pleased to hear again someday.

Questions for Group Discussion or Individual Reflection

Chapter 6: The Influence of Our Words

1. The author recalls a brief conversation he had with a newly drafted NBA player, Grant Hill, and the impact those words had on Hill. Have you ever had a similar experience, in which a few words someone said to you had a huge impact on your life? Or have other people told you that a few words you said impacted them in a big way?

   How did that experience make you feel? How has it influenced the things you say and the way you live your life?

2. The author describes a conversation with his sister Ruth in which she says, "Growing up, nobody ever told me I looked nice." Are there people in your sphere of influence who may have been looking to you for affirmation and you haven't even realized it? The affirmation they seek may not be in the area of attractiveness—they may hunger for affirmation that they are competent, accepted, or loved. Who comes to mind? What kind of affirmation does that person need? What steps can you take, beginning right now, to offer the words that person needs to hear?

3. The author tells how Coach Mike Holmgren, entrepreneur Herb Kelleher, and first lady Betty Ford all had a greater influence because they were committed to *telling the truth*—even when the truth might cost them or reveal flaws in their public image. What lessons do you draw for your own life from their example? Do you find it easy or difficult to be truthful in all your interactions with others? When you "shade the truth" or tell a lie, who are you really trying to protect—the other person or yourself? What steps do you need to take, starting right now, to build a strong foundation of truth for your life?

4. Do you ever engage in gossip? If so, why? What motivates you to talk about other people behind their backs? Is gossip ever justified?

Have you ever experienced or witnessed a situation in which gossip created great harm to you or someone else? How does that experience affect your view of gossip?

The author suggests a seven-question test we should take before spreading information about another person:

1. Am I going to harm someone's reputation?
2. Am I willing to go straight to that person and discuss the matter privately?
3. Is the person I'm telling in a position to deal with the matter?
4. Am I betraying someone's trust? If so, do I have a good reason for doing so?
5. Am I willing to be identified as the source of the story?
6. Are my motives pure—and am I seeking attention or trying to hurt someone?
7. Am I obeying the Golden Rule?

Does this test seem useful and practical for your life? Explain how this test would (or would not) help you. If gossip is a temptation for you, what steps can you take to control your impulse to talk about others?

7

Be a Parent of Influence

> The words spoken by parents to their children in
> the privacy of home . . . are like words spoken in a
> whispering-gallery, and will be clearly heard at the
> distance of years, and along the corridors of ages
> that are yet to come.
>
> Dr. John Cumming, *Prophetic Studies*, 1854[1]

Recently my wife, Ruth, and I were talking in the kitchen while babysitting our three-year-old grandson, Anthony. This little guy was sitting in his tiny rocking chair. I remembered I needed to get something out of my car, so I walked out of the kitchen and headed for the door, when I heard a little voice behind me:

"Poppers, where are you going?"

I turned, and there was Anthony, my little shadow, looking up at me. "I'm going to my car, Anthony," I said.

"Can I follow you?"

"Sure, Anthony, sure."

So he followed me to the car. I retrieved the things I needed, then locked up the car. Again, I heard that little voice behind me.

"Poppers," Anthony said, "can I follow you all the time?"

"Sure you can, Anthony."

"Wherever you go?"

"Yes, Anthony. Wherever I go."

And as I said those words, I was overwhelmed with a very strong emotion that brought a lump to my throat. The feelings seemed to come out of nowhere—but they were stirred by the realization of the joy—and the responsibility—of having an influence on future generations.

Whether you are a parent or a grandparent, it's a sobering thing to realize that there are young people who are watching you, who are asking, "Can I follow you? Can I follow you all the time? Wherever you go?" Novelist James Baldwin put it this way: "The situation of our youth is not mysterious. Children have never been good at listening to their elders, but they have never failed to imitate them."[2]

My wife was raised in the gracious South, in Louisiana and Mississippi. She's a true southern lady, and her mother taught her an important lesson early in life: Never leave the house unless you are looking your best. Ruth has taken her mother's advice to heart throughout her life. She never goes anywhere, not even to Starbucks on a Saturday morning, unless she is well-dressed, her makeup in place, and her hair coiffed. No, you won't find her at the hardware store in an evening gown—but you also won't find her there in bib overalls. She's always dressed perfectly for every situation.

I learned about this trait in Ruth soon after we were married. We began running marathons together—twelve in all, including three Boston Marathons. The Boston Marathon is a long but scenic slog through several Massachusetts villages and towns. We always experience a sense of triumph as we conquer Heartbreak Hill, head down Beacon Street, and make that last turn onto Boylston Street for the final push.

But right after rounding that corner, Ruth always stops, reaches into her fanny pack, and pulls out her lipstick and comb. She checks her hair, makes sure her makeup is perfect—then we push on to the finish line. Along that final stretch, the photographers are lined up, snapping at everything that moves. Ruth might be the only woman in history to run marathons fully made up.

Why does she do it? Because of her mother's influence. She can hear her mother's voice in her mind, saying, "Never leave the house unless you are looking your best." A parent's influence lasts a lifetime. As parents, you and I need to make sure that we are influencing our kids in the right direction.

Parents of Healthy Influence

All of our nineteen sons and daughters have left home. They've gone off to college, to careers, to the Marine Corps, and to start their own families. But there was a time (and I shudder to remember it) when I had sixteen teenagers living under my roof at the same time. So when I speak on the subject of parenting, I think I speak with at least a modicum of authority.

What do I mean when I say, "Be a parent of influence"? Clearly, the word *parent* does not mean "biological progenitor" in my mind.

I have been in the delivery room to welcome four birth-children into the Williams clan. I have cradled each one in my hands as the doctor cut the cord—then I kissed them and blessed them and helped name them. I have also stood in the airport terminal to welcome fourteen adopted children into the Williams clan. I have watched big jet planes swoop down from South Korea, the Philippines, Romania, and Brazil, and every time a plane landed, our family expanded. I have kissed and blessed each one of those fourteen kids, and I have helped name them. I have looked into the faces of all my many children, and I have prayed for each one and have told them about the loving Lord who has a wonderful future planned for them.

The vast majority of my kids are connected to me by love, not genetics. And a parent's love is both stronger and vastly more important than biology. To me, a "parent" is anyone who has the spiritual and emotional capacity to love and nurture a child. So a "parent" could be a birth parent, adoptive parent, stepparent, grandparent, or godparent. Whether or not you ever have birth children, you can have a loving, nurturing influence—a *parental* influence—in the life of a child.

A few years ago, I was in Boston on a promotional tour for my book on the life of Michael Jordan. That morning, I did an interview for a local TV talk show. That night, I went to the Fleet Center, to see Michael Jordan and the Washington Wizards play the Boston Celtics. Before the game, I went down to the locker room and chatted with Mike.

"Hey, I saw you on TV this morning," he said. "You know, you're telling all my stories in that book!"

"Mike," I said, "your stories are getting rave reviews from people all around the country. They write and say, 'When you see Michael Jordan, thank him for being a good influence on our kids.'"

"I'm just a product of my mom and dad," he replied. "I owe everything I am to James and Deloris Jordan and all the things they taught me."

That's a powerful tribute to the impact of parents who take their influence seriously. As parents, we lay a foundation for our children's lives through our words and actions. This doesn't mean we can completely control how our kids will turn out. They are subject to influences from peers, school, the media, and the culture around them. Some young people reject the solid foundation their parents have provided for them, and we cannot blame the parents for that. But as a general rule, parents of healthy influence tend to produce children who are emotionally and spiritually healthy.

I'm a deeply flawed human being—flawed as a husband, as a father, and as a Christian. I am the father of nineteen flawed human beings. Here in the vast Williams household, we've had our share of conflicts and problems. But no matter how rocky things got when our kids were all growing up together, there was always a nucleus of love, faith, and commitment that bonded us. I like to think that our miniature United Nations succeeded as well as it did because we as parents were committed (in spite of our limitations and mistakes) to living out the impact of parental influence.

Here are some nuggets of wisdom I have acquired (often by trial and error) while helping to shepherd nineteen souls from childhood through adolescence to young adulthood:

1. Influence by Blessing and Affirming

"My father told me about a month before he died that he was very proud of me," said retired NBA star Bill Russell. "And that is the biggest compliment I could ever imagine, 'cause he was my hero. And I was proud of him."[3]

There are few greater ways to bless and affirm your children than by saying, "I'm proud of you." Whether they succeed or fail, be proud of them. When they succeed, tell them you knew they could do it. When they fail, tell them you know that they will recover and achieve great things. Always tell your children you believe in them. Prophesy a great future for them. Let them know that you accept them and love them unconditionally.

Child psychologists Michael Thompson and Dan Kindlon tell the story of Raul, a father who took his six-year-old boy skiing. The boy fell, picked himself up, fell again, and generally struggled with getting the hang of skiing. But his father encouraged his son and cheered him on no matter how many times he did a face-plant in the snow. When it was time to head back to the lodge, Raul asked his boy what he enjoyed most about their time on the ski slopes. The boy replied, "Watching you watch me ski!"

Thompson and Kindlon conclude, "What really mattered to the boy was not how well or poorly he skied but what his dad thought of him. So it is with most boys in middle childhood: their opinion about whether they are competent depends on how they think their father sees them."[4]

The Bible tells us that it is a privilege and a duty for parents to bless their children, and for grandparents to bless their grandchildren:

> By faith Isaac blessed Jacob and Esau in regard to their future.
> By faith Jacob, when he was dying, blessed each of Joseph's sons, and worshiped as he leaned on the top of his staff.
>
> Hebrews 11:20–21

Isaac, the father of Jacob and Esau, told his sons that God had prepared a great future for them. And Jacob, the father of Joseph, told his grandsons that they, too, were blessed by God. Have you influenced your children and grandchildren with the impact of your blessing? Have you told them about the love of God, and about God's wonderful plan for their future?

"I'm proud of you! I believe in you! I'm on your side!" Those words have an incalculable impact on the heart and mind of an approval-hungry child.

2. Influence by Investing Your Time

Jim Brozina is a retired school librarian in Millville, New Jersey. His wife left him when his daughter, Kristen, was ten years old. At around the same time, Kristen's older sister left for college. So it was a tough time for Jim as he tried to support his daughter Kristen through a time of losses. Jim worried that he and Kristen might begin to drift apart. So he came up with an idea he now calls The Streak.

Jim suggested they set a goal of reading together every night for a hundred consecutive nights. Father and daughter had been reading together since Kristen was little—but they read sporadically, not as a nightly commitment. Jim set some rules for The Streak: They had to read at least one complete chapter of a book each night, and they had to be finished before the stroke of midnight, or it wouldn't count.

Kristen agreed and they read every night, beginning with *The Wizard of Oz* by L. Frank Baum. At the end of a hundred nights, they decided to keep The Streak going. After two hundred nights, they were still going. Then three hundred nights, then four hundred, and on and on.

When Kristen went into high school, she and her dad were still reading together every night—and The Streak was still going strong. Instead of children's books, however, they were reading Shakespeare's *King Lear*.

If Kristen was at a party with her high school friends, she'd ask one of them to drive her home so her dad could read with her. (Kristen didn't drive.) The Streak even continued right through prom night. "Before I went out," she recalled, "I had my hair in my up-do and my fancy dress on. And I just sort of climbed into the bed next to him and he read to me."

The Streak continued until Kristen went away to college. Jim Brozina drove his daughter to the Rutgers campus, Kristen moved her belongings into the dorm—then father and daughter sat on the steps of the dorm stairwell and read together one last time before calling a halt to The Streak. They read from the book that had begun The Streak—*The Wizard of Oz*.

"That was the single hardest thing to do," Jim Brozina said later, "to read, choked up, tears in our eyes—both of us." Had it been hard to keep The Streak going? No, Jim said, the hardest thing was bringing it to an end. The Streak had lasted 3,218 days—almost nine years.

"He put in every night for years," Kristen recalled. "He didn't have to do that. He's selfless."[5]

Not surprisingly, Kristen graduated with a degree in English literature, and went on to write a book about her father's nightly commitment to reading with her. The book is called *The Reading Promise: My Father and the Books We Shared*. I suggest you read it—but don't look for the name Kristen Brozina on the cover. She has taken the name Alice Ozma. To find out why

Kristen changed her name to Alice, read her book. (You won't get any spoilers from me!)

How do children spell "love"? They spell it T-I-M-E. To have a significant influence on your children, you must spend a significant amount of time with them. You have to make a conscious commitment of your time and attention—and the busier you are, the more serious you must be about keeping that time commitment with your kids.

Years ago, I was on a committee that helped make the case to Dr. Bill Bright that he and his organization, Campus Crusade for Christ, should move their headquarters from California to Orlando. Shortly after Campus Crusade made the move to central Florida, Dr. Bright and his wife Vonette invited us to their home for dinner. In the course of our conversation, Bill asked about all of our children. (At that point, there were eighteen children in the Williams household.) His question was essentially, "How do you do it? How do you make it work?"

I immediately began to talk about the discipline we instilled, the rules and regulations in our family, and the penalties we imposed for violating the rules. Bill listened carefully and quietly. Then, in that calm and understated way of his, he simply said, "Don't forget the love."

That was good advice. In the course of trying to keep our family system functioning like a fine-tuned machine, it was easy to forget the most important ingredient in any family. Rules and structure are important, but *love* is the glue that holds everything together.

Along with the love, a family must have *fun*. One day at the dinner table, I was giving the kids one of my lectures when Kati—one of the two little girls we had adopted from Romania—put up her hand up and said, "Dad! Dad! Why can't you just be a casual dad?"

We had adopted Kati when she was five, and by this time she was about eight. I said, "Kati, what is your definition of a 'casual dad'?"

She said, "Casual dads have *fun* with their children."

Ooh, that hurt! I had regimented my kids. I had given them rules and structure. But I had not been having *fun* with my kids lately.

After that reminder from Kati, I became more conscious of my need to be a "casual dad," a *fun* dad. I became more aware of the crucial importance of *fun* in our family.

We should spend learning time, relationship-building time, and faith-building time with our children. But above all, we need to spend *fun* time with our children, because everything else we do together—learning, growing closer, and growing deeper in our faith—can be done in an atmosphere of fun. Make a game out of learning. Go to exciting places together—the zoo, the aquarium, or the natural history museum. Take your kids to an amusement park and use the roller-coaster ride to teach your children about the joy of adventure and confidence-building.

Dr. Michael Thompson recalls taking his six-year-old son Will on a drive through the Green Mountains of Vermont. The road was windy, and a fierce thunderstorm whipped up, lashing the windshield with sheets of rain. Lightning flashed and thunder exploded around them as they drove. Dr. Thompson realized that if the downpour and lightning made him—a grownup—feel anxious, how must Will feel? Checking the rearview mirror, he saw the boy strapped into his car seat, wide-eyed with fear.

Though the storm was violent, it didn't last long. After the weather calmed down, Dr. Thompson wanted to help Will express his fears. He rejected the question, *You weren't scared, were you, buddy?* Such a question would only encourage Will to deny his feelings. So Dr. Thompson said, "That was a little scary, wasn't it, Will?"

"No, Dad," said the boy. "That was *very* scary."[6]

Special moments like these only happen when we as parents are spending time with our kids, going places and doing things with them, drawing out their feelings, and listening to them. Our influence with our children begins with an investment of our time.

Listening to our children is a powerful and much-neglected relationship-building strategy. It's so easy to *pretend* we are listening, when we are really just waiting for them to stop talking. We say, "Uh-huh. . . . Oh, really? . . . That's nice." But our kids can tell when they're being patronized. They feel devalued when they know we aren't listening. And once these moments have flown, we can never get them back. When investing time in our kids, let's invest our full attention. That means making eye contact, listening, giving verbal feedback, and enjoying those fleeting moments when we can influence their lives.

3. Influence through Consistent Discipline

Dr. Vincent Mumford is an associate professor of physical education and sports at Central Michigan University in Mount Pleasant, Michigan. I became acquainted with Dr. Mumford when he held a similar position at the University of Central Florida. He once told me a story about the disciplinary style of his mother.

"No one taught character like my mother," he said. "I was the team captain and starting guard on my junior varsity basketball team. One night my mother told me to do the dishes. I was tired, so I figured I'd do my chores later—but I fell asleep and never got around to the dishes.

"The next day, my mother informed me that there were consequences to my actions—and she wouldn't let me play basketball. That was embarrassing! I had to go to school and tell my coach what happened. He came to my house after school and spoke to my mother, but she wouldn't budge. Not only did I miss a game, but I was ridiculed by my teammates. She let me rejoin the team after that one-game suspension—and I learned a valuable lesson: I was accountable to the team—and to my mother."

Children need to know that we mean what we say and we say what we mean. If we promise to ground them for breaking our rules, we need to follow through. And if we promise to take them to Disney World as a reward for good behavior, we need to keep that promise as well. When our children learn that we are consistent, reasonable people who act in predictable, dependable ways, they will feel secure and loved, knowing exactly where the boundary lines are.

Kids need limits. They crave structure—even when they rebel against it. Children need limits on TV, computer games, and other entertainment, and they need a set time for doing home-work. They need to have a consistent bedtime that allows them to get adequate sleep. Be consistent. Be firm. Be loving. And *be the parent.*

When the Williams family had so many kids living under one roof, we had a number of important rules in our family. Those rules were tested on a fairly frequent basis, so discipline was an important part of my job as the father of all those kids. When we correct children, it's important to do so in a calm and controlled frame of mind—never in anger.

What if your child becomes disrespectful during a heated argument? Treat it as a "teachable moment." Stop the con-versation and tell the child, "I'm willing to listen to you, but I won't allow you to treat me with disrespect. Would you like to restate what you just said, but in a respectful way?" This gives the child the opportunity to correct his own behavior, and he learns he can express the same thoughts and feelings in a constructive way. Learning to handle disagreements without being obnoxious and hurtful is an important step in a child's character development.

If you feel angry and you don't think you can control your words or your actions, then it's time for both sides to take a time-out. Send your kids to their room while you sit down, take a walk, do some deep breathing, pray, and carefully consider your next move. If you lose your temper, you will likely lose control of the situation—and that's why kids often try to provoke their parents. When you remain cool, calm, and rational, you prove that you are in control.

I like to use the analogy of a traffic cop. When a police officer stops you for speeding, does he get mad and start yelling at you? Of course not. Traffic cops are unfailingly polite. They call you "Sir" or "Ma'am," and they speak to you calmly but firmly. After handing you a ticket that's going to cost you hundreds of dollars, they inexplicably yet politely say, "Have a nice day." Why are police officers always so cool and calm? It's because they are trained to maintain a calm demeanor to keep the public calm and to demonstrate that they control the situation.

If you have to "arrest" your children's behavior, take a lesson from the traffic cop. Keep your voice low and your emotions in check. Even if your kids are out of control, let them know that you are in command.

A number of years ago, I had to discipline one of my teenage sons by taking away some of his privileges. It was a rough patch in our father-son relationship—but we got through it. And after my son had taken some time to reflect on the things he had done to bring these consequences on himself, he sat down, handwrote a note to me, and left it by my place at the table. He had written:

Dad,
I am sorry for all the troubles I've caused. It will never happen again. I understand why you are mad at me. Please forgive me. I know you're trying to help me understand what life is all about.
Thank you for being hard on me.

Love, [his name here]

Well, I was disappointed, but I wasn't "mad" at him. And after I read that note, we had a great talk and a wonderful reconciliation. One heartwarming note like this one can make up for a lot of teenager-induced heartburn. This wasn't the last time the two of us butted heads, nor the last time he apologized. We got through it, and the father-son bond between us is stronger than ever today.

4. Influence by Teaching Your Kids to Work Hard and Serve Others

Give your children plenty of opportunities to build character by serving others. Encourage your kids to put down the iPads and game controllers, and to get involved in the *real* world around them. Suggest that they wash windows or pull weeds for an elderly neighbor—not to make money, but to make a difference. Encourage them to write a letter to a soldier overseas to thank them for the work they do to keep America safe. Suggest that they volunteer to serve meals at a rescue mission or homeless shelter, or to help build houses with Habitat for Humanity. Help your kids discover the joy of service to others—not for applause or pay, but simply for the joy of serving God and others.

If your kids are a little timid or reluctant, offer to go with them and volunteer your own time along with them. You may wonder at times if all the trouble it takes to train and motivate your kids is worth it. But keep loving them, keep investing in their lives, and one day you'll know that you have invested wisely. You'll know that you've made a difference in their lives—and you've made a difference in the world.

After the publication of my 2005 book *Coaching Your Kids to Be Leaders*, I received an email from a reader named Tom Walsh. He wrote, "Thanks for writing this book! As a father of two boys, ages two and four (with a third child on the way), I found a lot of ideas in your book about how to raise emotionally and spiritually healthy kids. Your book inspired me to action."

Then he told me about taking his two boys out to a bagel store for a Saturday morning breakfast. After that, they went to a nearby convalescent home to visit the residents. Tom wasn't sure of the procedures for visiting the residents, so he went to the front desk and told the receptionist that they had come to visit someone.

"What is the name of the resident?" the receptionist asked.

Tom said, "Anyone. We just want to visit someone who needs some company."

The staff allowed Tom and his two sons to wander around the facility and talk to anyone. At last, Tom and his boys came to a lounge where a number of residents were having coffee and doughnuts. Tom's four-year-old, George, walked up to people, extended his hand, and said, "Hi! I'm George! It's nice to meet you!"

The residents were charmed by Tom's two boys—and for the boys, it was the first of many such experiences. Tom concluded, "You can never start too early training kids to serve others. At the same time, you're teaching them to sharpen their social skills and overcome their shyness. Thanks again for providing that spark of inspiration!"

Tom's story inspired me—and I hope it has inspired an idea or two that you can put into practice with your own kids. What a great way to impact others in a positive way while having a powerful, life-changing influence on your children!

5. Influence by Teaching and Modeling Good Character

To instill good character traits in our children, our actions must match our words. Susy Flory has coauthored several books, including *So Long Status Quo*, and has written for such publications as *In Touch*, *Praise & Coffee*, and *Today's Christian Woman*. I asked Susy to name the most important role model of integrity and character in her life.

"My father," she said. "He demonstrated integrity in every aspect of his life. Every Sunday night he was in the habit of paying bills and reconciling his budget at his big desk upstairs in the bedroom. During bill-paying time, he always treated himself to a cigar or a pipe. Whenever I smelled that sweet tobacco scent, I knew where he was.

"One Sunday night I followed the scent of smoke and came upon him writing a check to Elmhurst Baptist Church, our home church, for $3,000. I said, 'Wow! That's a lot of money!'

"He explained, 'Last year, money was really tight and I got behind on my tithe. Now I'm making up for it.' We were a middle-class family, not wealthy by any measure, and no one would have known if he had skipped those tithes. But he knew and he lived up to his commitment to tithe ten percent without fail. That made a big impression on me."

My friend, retired Florida State head football coach Bobby Bowden, told me that he, too, learned lessons in character as a child while learning about tithing. He said, "My mother taught me the most about character. For example, she wanted me to learn generosity and faithfulness to God, so she started early teaching me to give a tenth to the Lord. When I was of grammar school age, she gave me a ten-cent allowance. She told me that one penny of that ten cents belonged to God, and I should put it in the offering at church. Year by year, she raised my allowance from ten cents to twenty, to thirty, and eventually to a dollar a week—and I faithfully tithed one tenth of my weekly allowance. Today, tithing tens of thousands of dollars a year is not a chore for me. Tithing is a natural part of my life because Mama taught me from my earliest years to give what belonged to God."

David Cutcliffe is currently the head football coach of the Duke University Blue Devils. David tells how his father taught good character to him and his siblings.

"My father died when I was fifteen," David said. "He worked hard, but we never had very much. There were six of us children plus the parents, all living in a home with one bathroom. Dad would often take us to the park for Sunday afternoon outings.

"One time we went to the park in our 1952 Chevrolet (I thought that car was a limousine), and we jumped out and played and played. When the other people at the park saw us coming, I'm sure they thought, 'Oh, gosh, the Cutcliffes are here.' But we had a great time at the park. At around dusk, when our day at the park was over, Dad whistled with his fingers in his mouth. If you heard that whistle, you knew that it was time to come running."

As the kids all headed for the car, David's father told them to wait. "He had us all sit down on one of those concrete picnic tables," David recalled. "'Look around,' he said. 'What do you see?'"

David and his siblings looked around them, but didn't know what they were supposed to see. "Do you see all of this trash here?" his father asked. "I want every single piece of trash picked up before we leave."

The Cutcliffe children protested, "But, Daddy, we didn't leave that trash."

But that didn't matter to David's father. "He had us pick up the trash in the park," David said, "and put it in those big fifty-five-gallon trash drums. There was so much trash, we filled up a couple of drums. Then he sat us down on the picnic table again, and he said, 'Look around.' We all looked, and even as a young child, I noticed how pretty the park looked, even in semidarkness. Then he said, 'I want you to remember something. Wherever you go, whatever you do, always remember: Cutcliffes leave it better than they found it.'"

That lesson has stuck with David Cutcliffe throughout his life.[7]

I once heard how a father gave an object lesson in character to his ten-year-old son. He took the boy out to the end of the block and showed him the lawn of the corner house. The grass at the corner was matted down and worn bare in places. "You see how the grass has been trampled down?" he said.

The son nodded.

"That's because people cut across the front lawn instead of staying on the sidewalk. What does that tell us about the people who take that shortcut? It tells us they are lazy. People who cut corners just to save themselves a few steps are building lazy habits that will follow them throughout their lives. They'll be the ones who cut corners with the truth and with their responsibilities. They'll build a bad reputation for cutting corners. If you want people to trust you, then you have to tell yourself, 'I don't cut corners. I don't do a halfway job. I go the extra mile.' If you stick to that decision for the rest of your life, people will see that in you. Your teachers, your coaches, and your employers will see something special in you. Your good character will give you an edge over all the run-of-the-mill people who cut corners."

That lesson was planted in that young man's mind for the rest of his life. Every time he saw the trampled-down corner of a lawn, he was reminded of a life lesson in maintaining good character.

A friend once told me, "When I was about twelve, my dad told me about something he had read—a test that an employer gave to every applicant who walked into his office for a job interview. The employer would crumple a piece of paper and toss it on the carpet. Then, when the applicant would walk into the office, the employer would see what that person would do. If the applicant ignored the crumpled paper, the job interview was over. But if the applicant picked up the crumpled paper and placed it in the waste basket, the interview would continue.

"The employer wanted to find out if the applicant was willing to do more than was expected of him—or if he would say, 'That's not my job.' My dad doesn't even remember telling me that story—it's been more than forty years since then. But I think of it every time I'm tempted to give a sloppy or halfhearted effort. That story has had a huge impact on my character."

Dr. Maxie Miller Jr. is the director of the African-American Ministries Division of the Florida Baptist Convention. He told me, "My parents were the fundamental force in my moral and spiritual development. God was at the center of everything they taught me. My role model has always been my dad.

"I remember my father sitting with me many evenings, answering my questions about life, from the time I was a young boy right into my adulthood. Not many fathers and sons have had as close a relationship as he and I have had. I respected his wisdom, and when Daddy didn't have the answer to my question, he'd ask our pastor for help in finding direction from the Scriptures.

"When I was in my second year of high school, I faced some strong peer pressure. My friends talked about sex and ridiculed guys who were not sexually active. I had just started dating, and I wanted to hear the truth about sex, so I went to my dad and we talked. He told me about being moral and responsible, having respect for the girls I dated, and how having sex outside of marriage can have a harmful effect on my life. He shared Scripture with me. I asked him, 'How did you handle this issue when you were my age?' He said simply, 'Your mother is the only woman I've ever been intimate with—and only after we were married.' That was all I needed to hear.

"The first new car our family owned was a 1968 Volkswagen. I was about seventeen when my father trusted me to take the car to have it serviced. He said, 'Don't give anyone else a ride in the car, go straight to school, and come straight home.' Well, I broke every one of those instructions. Somewhere between school and the service shop, I had an accident in the car with some of my friends inside. No one was hurt—but I had acted irresponsibly. After the accident, I drove around for most of the evening, wondering how I was going to explain the damage to my parents. Finally, I walked into the house and told my dad exactly what had happened.

"He said, 'I trusted you, and you let me down. You will work and pay for the repairs.' My mother was irate—she wanted a much harsher punishment. But Dad had already done the one thing that pierced me to the heart more than any punishment they could devise. He said, 'You let me down.' Because of my love and respect for my dad, I had terrible remorse for disappointing him. That was the greatest lesson in character I ever learned, and I often think of it to this day."

Jon Daniels, athletic director at Bethany College in Lindsborg, Kansas, told me, "When I was a boy, I went with my father to the bank to get a check cashed so we could go on a small vacation. When the teller counted out the money to my dad, she gave him way too much—at least a hundred dollars too much, and maybe a thousand, I don't remember the figure. But I do remember we didn't have much money in those days. Anyone in our circumstances would be tempted to take the money and not say a word about it. But that thought never entered my father's mind.

"He tried to get the teller's attention without letting her supervisor know what she had done—he didn't want to get the teller in trouble. He had to explain to her three or four times, 'No, I'm saying you gave me *too much* money. I'm trying to give some of it back.' Finally, she caught on and took the money back, and we left the bank.

"After we left the bank, my father explained to me what had happened and why it would have been stealing to keep the extra money, even though it was the teller's mistake. He always tried to use moments like that to teach me life lessons in character and faith. That happened forty years ago, and I still remember it vividly."

Arun Gandhi of Durban, South Africa, is a grandson of Mohandas K. Gandhi, the leader of India's nonviolent independence movement. Arun grew up under apartheid in South Africa, where he was often beaten by whites for being black, and by blacks for being too white. Embittered by the persecution he suffered, he sought revenge—until he learned from his father and grandfather the difference between justice and revenge. He discovered that the best way to be rid of an enemy is to convert him into a friend. Today, Arun goes around the world speaking to audiences about peacemaking.

I once shared a platform with Arun Gandhi at a National Speakers Association convention. He told a story from his teenage years in South Africa. His father had given him the family car and had instructed him, "Take the car to the repair shop, then you may go to the movie. But make sure you pick me up at five."

Arun agreed. After getting the car serviced, he went to the theater to watch a movie. The theater was showing a double feature, and though the second feature wouldn't be over until almost six, Arun decided to disobey his father and stay for the second film. He arrived an hour late to pick up his father. His father got in the car, and they started for home—about an eighteen-mile trip. There was an uncomfortable silence as Arun drove.

Finally, Arun's father said, "Why are you so late?"

"The car was not out of the shop yet," the boy lied. "I had to wait for it."

"Stop the car."

"Why, Father?"

"I'm walking home the rest of the way. I have failed as a father. I raised a son who lies. I called the garage, and they told me you picked up the car several hours ago."

Arun pulled the car over and his father got out and began walking. Night fell as he walked the entire distance—a five-hour walk. Arun couldn't bear to leave his father alone on the road, so he followed slowly in the car. The experience impacted Arun deeply, and he swore to himself that he would never again tell a lie. Watching his father walk all the way home from town was a lesson in character he would never forget.

As parents, we have a duty to shape the character of our children—and we impact and influence their character with our words and our example.

A Reward from God

In 1988, our family adopted four Filipino brothers, ages four through nine. After we brought them home, we gave them one day to rest—then we threw them right into a wide array of challenging experiences. With each new challenge, they balked and protested, "We've never done that before!"

For example, we took them to the pool at nearby Rollins College and handed them over to swim coach Harry Meisel and his son, Kevin. "But we can't swim!" all four boys said. They were right—but they learned. Harry and Kevin challenged those boys to attempt something they thought was impossible, and soon they couldn't wait to get into the pool. Within a few years, three of those brothers qualified for the Florida Junior Olympics and joined the ranks of the top youth swimmers in the state. It was amazing to watch the change in those boys.

At the height of our parenting adventure, when we had sixteen teenagers under one roof, our breakfast table was sixteen feet long. We served breakfast at six thirty, and I always tried to fire up the brain cells of my teenage herd before they stampeded out the door. I did this by posing a "question of the day."

One morning I said, "Twenty years from now, what will you remember most about your old dad?" The kids broke up into buzz groups and discussed the question for half a minute, then David (who was then sixteen, and later became a United States Marine) acted as spokesman for the group. "Dad," he said, "we decided that the thing we will always remember about you is that you were always motivating us."

Aha! I was getting through to them! That was one of my top goals—to motivate my teens to work hard in school, to do their chores without complaint or being nagged, to keep their rooms picked up, and to stay out of trouble. Today, my kids are scattered across this country, from California to New York to Florida. They're adults now—but my mission is the same. I still mail and email newspaper stories and quotations to them to encourage and motivate them.

I once heard about a mother of thirteen children who was asked by an interviewer, "Do you think all children deserve impartial love and attention from their parents?"

"Of course they do," she said.

"Well, which of your children do you love the most?" the interviewer asked, hoping to catch her in a contradiction.

She said, "The one who is sick, until he gets well, and the one who is away, until he gets home."

Ruth and I know how that mother feels. When people ask me how many children I have, I say, "Nineteen—four birth kids, one by remarriage, and fourteen by adoption—but I forget which fourteen."

So forgive me if I seem a bit fanatical about the subject of parenting and influencing kids. I just can't think of anything more important in this world than the calling from God to bless and love and nurture the next generation.

Solomon once observed, "Sons are a heritage from the Lord, children a reward from him" (Psalm 127:3). He also wrote, "Train a child in the way he should go, and when he is old he will not turn from it" (Proverbs 22:6). Whether you are a biological parent, adoptive parent, godparent, stepparent, or mentor, children are a reward from God. Cherish that reward. Disciple those children. Train them, coach them, encourage them, and influence them.

My youngest son, Alan, is now twenty-six. He was not the easiest kid to raise, and he will readily acknowledge that fact. He is a great young man with a good heart, but he's always been easily influenced, and he's made a few left turns from time to time.

Alan lives in Southern California, and he called me the other day. His first words came as quite a shock: "Dad, thanks for raising me the right way!"

"Alan," I said, "what brings this up? Has something happened?"

"Well, Dad, I've been having some problems with my girlfriend. But I remember everything you taught me. I'm not losing my temper. I'm handling everything the way you said I should. I've been thinking a lot about the lessons you tried to teach us—you know, all those lessons about character and maturity. And I think I'm getting it now. That stuff really works!"

I sat there openmouthed and amazed, hardly able to believe the sounds that were coming out of my phone. Oh, it was sweet music to a father's ears!

That's the ultimate tribute to any parent—to know that your attempts to influence your children have not been wasted. You don't expect those lessons to get through to them when they are young and headstrong, but you do hope that, somewhere down the road, your words will come back to them when needed.

I still get a tingle up my spine when I remember Alan's words: "Dad, thanks for raising me the right way." I hope you get to hear similar words someday, and that you experience that same tingle of joy.

The rewards that come with impacting the lives of our children don't just last a lifetime. They last forever.

Questions for Group Discussion or Individual Reflection

Chapter 7: Be a Parent of Influence

1. Did you grow up feeling blessed and affirmed by your parents or primary caregivers? How has the influence of your parents impacted your life? What are some specific examples of your parents' influence and the way their influence continues to shape your life today?

2. Is it easy for you to spend time with your children, or does it take a great deal of thought, effort, and schedule juggling to make it happen? Do you and your children have fun together? Can you think of specific ways you can change your life or adjust your schedule to make more time for your children?

3. Is it easy or difficult for you to discipline your children in a consistent way? Do you tend to discipline according to consistent principles and family rules—or according to your emotions at the moment?

   Is it easy or difficult for you to admit that you were wrong? What life lessons are your children learning from the way you deal with your own failings and mistakes? How does the author's explanation of Proverbs 22:6 ("Train a child in the way he should go") affect your view of discipline?

4. How are you teaching your children to value hard work and serving others? Give specific examples of actions you are taking with your children. The author offers a number of suggested activities to teach children the joy of serving others: washing windows, pulling weeds, serving meals, and so forth. Can you think of other activities your children could do to serve others?

5. What kind of role models were your parents? Do you remember learning character lessons by watching them respond to pressure, temptation, or other situations?

   What kind of lessons do you think your children are learning from your example?

8

Be a Leader of Influence

Socrates had a student named "Plato." Plato had
a student named "Aristotle." And Aristotle had a
student named "Alexander the Great."

Tom Morris, author of *If Aristotle
Ran General Motors*[1]

Former major league shortstop Alvin Dark is a good friend
of mine. Whenever I'm in his neck of the woods, I visit
Alvin and his wife, Jackie. After every visit, I feel I've gained
some new nuggets of wisdom.

On one occasion, I sat with Alvin and his wife, and I asked
him to share with me the most important lesson he learned as
a baseball manager. I had my pen poised, and I took down his
reply word for word. He said, "Here is a prayer I've tried to live
by as a manager: 'Lord, when I'm wrong, make me willing to
change. When I'm right, make me easy to live with. Strengthen
me so that the power of my example far exceeds the authority of my rank.' Pat, I have always tried to remember that you
manage by influence—not by authority."

159

I left Alvin Dark's home that afternoon knowing he had shared with me an influence principle for the ages: Whether you are a baseball manager, a military leader, a CEO, a pastor, a teacher, or a parent, you manage by the impact of your influence, not by your title, the stripes on your uniform, the degrees after your name, or your intimidating personality.

Authentic leadership is about influencing others—not being "the boss."

Meeting the Troops

Leadership expert John C. Maxwell writes, "Leadership is influence—nothing more, nothing less."[2] James C. Hunter, in *The World's Most Powerful Leadership Principle*, explains why leadership equals influence:

> Leadership is influencing people to willingly, even enthusiastically, contribute their hearts, minds, creativity, excellence, and other resources toward mutually beneficial goals. Leadership is influencing people to commit to the mission. Leadership is influencing people to become the best they are capable of becoming. Accordingly, leadership is *not* synonymous with management. Leadership is synonymous with influence.[3]

So it's important that leaders understand their role as influencers, and that they filter every decision through the template of their influence on others. Leaders need to ask themselves, "How will my actions affect other people, and my own reputation? Will these actions enhance or tarnish my moral reputation? Will these actions align with my values—or expose my hypocrisy?" If leadership truly is influence, as Maxwell, Blanchard, and Hunter tell us, then it's vitally important that we be intensely aware of the impact of our words and the influence of our actions.

James C. Shaffer, author of *The Leadership Solution*, has made an in-depth study of leaders and the organizations they lead, and he's discovered why so many individual stores or hotels within a chain seem to have a unique and distinct personality:

> Go to any grocery store that's part of a large national chain, and you'll see how the store manager's personality can be felt everywhere. The store's performance will be tracked closely with the quality of store management. Stay in a Hilton, Holiday Inn, Marriott, or Ritz Carlton. The general manager's presence is everywhere. It takes on his or her personality. The great grocery and lodging chains know this and invest huge amounts of time, energy, and money developing their store managers and general managers.
>
> People watch what leaders say and what they don't say, what they do and how they act. . . . We watch their body language. We note their tone of voice and facial expressions. We pay close attention to what they wear, who they promote, who they ignore. Everything a leader says and does is scrutinized for meaning, because everything a leader says or does assumes importance as a form of communication, often far beyond even what the leader imagines.[4]

Second Lieutenant Colin Powell, United States Army, was one of sixteen thousand military advisors sent to Vietnam by President Kennedy in 1962. There he was wounded by a punji-stick booby trap while on patrol in 1963. He was later injured in a helicopter crash and received a commendation for rescuing other soldiers from the burning helicopter in spite of his own injuries. He went on to earn an MBA at George Washington University, attained a White House fellowship, and served in various capacities in the administrations of Presidents Nixon, Carter, Reagan, Clinton, and George W. Bush. He was chairman of the Joint Chiefs of Staff under President George H. W. Bush, gaining national recognition during Operation Desert Storm. He served as secretary of state—at that time, the highest rank ever attained by an African American in the U.S. government.

"Leadership," Powell once said, "is motivating people, turning people on, getting 110 percent out of a personal relationship."[5]

In other words, leadership is influence. One of the ways Colin Powell has used his leadership influence is by spending time with his troops. In the summer of 1993, Powell—who was the then-chairman of the Joint Chiefs—flew to Somalia to be with the U.S. troops who were stationed there. He made twenty-three stops in a single twenty-hour period, telling a reporter for *Life* magazine, "Meeting the troops—that's what it's all about."

At each stop, General Powell would wade into a sea of GIs, shaking hands and posing for pictures with his men. Why did Powell think it was so important that he personally go out into the field and meet these soldiers face-to-face? He said that his commitment goes back to a visit he made to the Old Soldiers Home in Washington. During that visit, Powell went from room to room and met veterans from World War II, Korea, and Vietnam. Again and again, these vets would proudly show him their faded snapshots that had been taken decades earlier. Each snapshot showed the soldier standing with his commanding officer. Powell concluded, "That picture they had taken forty years ago with their general was the high point of their lives."[6]

General Powell wanted to make sure that the soldiers who fought on his watch got to experience that same high point in their lives. He was committed to using his leadership position to impact and influence his troops in a positive way.

A half century of leadership experience and study throughout my career has led me to conclude that leadership consists essentially of seven ways we influence others. I call them the Seven Sides of Leadership. They are:

1. *Vision*. Great leaders have a vision of a brighter tomorrow, and they seek to influence their team or organization toward the fulfillment of that vision.
2. *Communication Skills*. Communication is an essential tool of influence. We influence our followers and the people around us by communicating our vision, our values, and our beliefs in an honest and persuasive way.

3. *People Skills.* To influence others, we must be equipped to encourage, empower, and motivate them to work together. People skills are vital influencing skills that can be learned and improved with practice.

4. *Character.* Good character is essential to your influence. People choose whether or not to trust your leadership and accept your influence based on the trustworthiness of your character.

5. *Competence.* People are willing to be led and influenced by those who have demonstrated their competence as leaders. The word *competence* encompasses the word *compete.* Your subordinates or players want to be assured that you, as their leader, can make them competitive and lead them to victory.

6. *Boldness.* To be leaders of influence, we must speak firmly and act decisively. As the apostle Paul once wrote, "For if the trumpet give an uncertain sound, who shall prepare himself to the battle?" (1 Corinthians 14:8, KJV). Boldness, courage, daring, and decisiveness are all qualities of a leader of influence.

7. *Servanthood.* Authentic leadership is not about bossing people around. It's about having a healthy influence on others through an attitude of humility and acts of service. Yes, a leader of influence must give orders and hold subordinates accountable—not in a domineering way, but in order to motivate subordinates to achieve their goals and fulfill their potential.

Some people are born with at least a few of these Seven Sides of Leadership, but I have never known anyone who was born with all seven. These are all learnable skills. They are traits that almost anyone can acquire with practice. We can grow in our ability to envision a better future; we can increase our communication and people skills; we can dedicate ourselves to deeper integrity and stronger character; we can accept risks and challenges that enable us to build our confidence and boldness;

and we can daily choose to adopt the attitude and habits of a servant. The more complete we are in all seven of these traits, the greater our influence will be.

Every leader is in the people business. Leadership is nothing more or less than the ability to achieve important goals by influencing a group of people to work together. Coaches influence players to train hard, play together, and win championships. CEOs influence organizations to increase return-on-investment, market share, and stock value. Political leaders seek to influence their constituents to support them, and seek to influence fellow politicians to cooperate on implementing policies that improve society. Military leaders influence the troops to work together to achieve victory.

If you want to gauge a leader's influence, simply measure the accomplishments of that leader's team or organization. The greater the results, the greater the influence.

Committed to Winning, Committed to Influence

One of the most enjoyable privileges of my life is that I get to emcee the Philadelphia Sports Hall of Fame induction dinner every year. It's been twenty-seven years since I left Philadelphia, but the Philly sports community still remembers me and brings me back for this event. One of the inductees at the November 2011 dinner was former linebacker Bill Bergey, who played for the Eagles from 1974 through 1980. Bergey had been a key factor in the rise of the Eagles during the 1970s, crowned by a trip to Super Bowl XV after the 1980 season.

Bergey's old coach, Dick Vermeil, was on hand to receive an award on behalf of former Eagles running back Wilbert Montgomery. Because of a last-minute cancellation, there was no one on hand to present the award to Bill Bergey. I took Dick Vermeil aside and asked him to fill in and introduce Bergey. Dick readily agreed, and I said, "Great—you've got about ten minutes to get ready."

So when the time came to induct Bergey, I called Dick Vermeil to the microphone. And while I was introducing Dick, I heard the sound of choking and sobbing next to me. I turned and looked at Dick, and he was standing there with tears running down his cheeks, shaking with emotion. Now, I have seen Dick Vermeil get emotional before—in 2005, when he gave a press conference announcing his retirement from coaching, he broke down and cried eight times in one hour. Sportswriter Rick Reilly once said that Dick has the emotional stability of Judy Garland. But Dick hadn't said one word—in fact, I hadn't finished introducing him—and there he was, melting into a puddle of tears.

He came to the microphone and, with his voice shaking, said, "You all know that I get very emotional. And Bill Bergey just brings tears to my eyes."

I looked around the room and it occurred to me that there is nothing that reaches the emotions of a bunch of sportswriters and aging athletes like seeing an old coach cry. Finally, Dick got his emotions under control (somewhat), and he was able to talk about Bergey—about the way Bergey anchored the Eagles defense and was the key factor in getting the team to Super Bowl XV. Finally, wiping away tears and racked with sobs, Dick concluded, "I love this guy, Bill Bergey."

When Bill came to the microphone, he was more controlled than Dick Vermeil—but you could see the emotion and the affection he had for his old coach. Bergey talked fondly about the impact Dick had on his career with the Eagles.

As I watched these two men pay tribute to each other, I thought, *Wow! Here we have one of the truly great coaches of the NFL and one of the truly great defensive players of the NFL—and you can see the impact and the influence they had on each other.* And Dick Vermeil has had that kind of influence with literally hundreds of players over the years. He's truly a seven-sided leader—and above all, he truly has a servant's heart, and a love for the men he has coached. That's why Dick Vermeil is a leader of influence.

A genuine leader of influence does not merely pursue his or her own goals and ambitions. A true person of influence is committed to mentoring, training, and equipping others to become leaders in their own right.

In December 2011, the *Wall Street Journal* profiled Hayden Fry, former head football coach at the University of Iowa (1979–1998), who compiled a career college coaching record of 232–178–10. Under his leadership, the *Journal* reported, Iowa became "a different sort of football factory—one that specializes in [producing] coaches." Fry's football program has produced more head coaches and assistants than any other Division I college football program.

Now in his eighties and retired from coaching, Hayden Fry gave an interview from his home in Mesquite, Nevada. He explained that his approach to influencing and training coaches was inspired by lessons he learned from his father, an Odessa, Texas, rancher. When Hayden was a boy, his father had him load the pickup with hay and drive out to feed the cows before school. "We have two thousand acres and creeks and trees," young Hayden told his dad. "How am I going to find all those cows?" His father replied, "All you have to do is drive out and listen. One cow is the leader, the bell cow. Find the bell cow, and you find the whole herd."

The bell cow became a metaphor to describe Fry's approach to finding and training coaches. He would look at his roster of players, identify certain ones who seemed to have the right mix of playing and teaching skills, the ones other players seemed to look to and follow—then he would try them out as player-coaches. Some didn't work out—but the ones who succeeded became Fry's assistant coaches. Creating a system of player-coaches worked well at Iowa because, as Fry put it, "those are the guys who players will listen to, not an old coach like me."

Fry brought many Iowa grads back into his program as graduate assistants. Many of his "bell cow" assistants liked coaching so much that they changed their life goals and made their careers in coaching. The *Journal* reported, "Several of Iowa's former assistants say Fry was a prolific mentor because he wouldn't hire an assistant unless he believed that assistant was capable of becoming a head coach some day."

And Fry himself said, "I think of these guys as my sons and I follow and watch them all. It makes you feel good, like you really made a difference in people's lives."[7] Spoken like an authentic leader of influence.

Bobby Jones was one of the outstanding players who lifted the Philadelphia 76ers to an NBA championship (1982–1983 season) when I was general manager. He's also the player who originated the idea of chapel services before NBA games. Bobby is a good friend and I've kept in touch with him over the years. A number of years ago, during the spectacular playing career of NFL defensive end Reggie White, Bobby told me about a conversation he had with Reggie at a Christian event where Bobby spoke. (Reggie White, of course, was the Green Bay Packers "Minister of Defense," the most dominant NFL pass rusher of his era; Reggie died unexpectedly in 2004 due to a complication from a chronic lung condition.)

After Bobby gave his speech, Reggie approached him and said, "Bobby, I want to thank you for the influence you've had on my life."

Bobby was surprised. "What do you mean?"

"When I was in junior high school," Reggie explained, "I went to a Fellowship of Christian Athletes camp. You spoke there, and your message impacted my life in a huge way. You even took some extra time individually with me at the camp. My favorite NBA team was the 76ers, and seeing the way you cared about kids—well, that had a big influence on me."

Reggie White went on to become a leader of Christian influence in his own right. My writing partner, Jim Denney, spent several days in 1996 interviewing Reggie and his wife, Sara, at their Knoxville, Tennessee, home. In the interview, conducted a few months before his Super Bowl championship season, Reggie talked at length about his coaches and the enormous impact they had on his life. Here are some of Reggie's reflections on the influence of the coaches he played for.

Reggie told Jim, "Good coaches, the ones who have a lasting impact on your life, are people you remember as long as you live." Reggie recalled the man who coached organized neighborhood baseball when he was in elementary school; this man would pick up Reggie and his teammates in a station wagon and drive them to games. Reggie also recalled his junior high baseball and football coaches, Big Doug and Buford. "They could get us boys motivated without cussing us," Reggie said. "They helped us see that in order to win games, we had to do things we didn't want to do, like running laps and mastering the fundamentals."

Reggie's high school coach in Chattanooga was Robert Pulliam, who was once a standout defensive lineman at the University of Tennessee in the early 1970s. "One time, Coach Pulliam asked me about my ambitions," Reggie recalled. "I said, 'I want to be a minister.' That surprised him—I don't think any high school kid ever told him that before. He told me, 'I really believe you could be the best defensive player to ever play the game of football.' I said, 'You mean, in high school?' He said, 'No, I mean in pro football.' To this day, I don't know what he saw in me, but when he said that, he inspired me to want to be the best at what I do."

Looking back, Reggie realized that, though Coach Pulliam saw great potential in him, he also spotted a weakness. To Coach Pulliam, Reggie was "a nice, big Sunday school boy who didn't want to hurt anybody."[8] If he sent Reggie out with orders to put a hit on someone, Reggie would do it—but within a play or two, he'd ease off. Coach Pulliam couldn't keep pulling Reggie to the sidelines to tell him how he was supposed to hit. So he came up with a plan to toughen Reggie up.

Reggie told Jim, "Coach Pulliam began to push me and harass me on the field and in the gym. It baffled me, because it really intensified after he told me how great I could become. He and I would rassle in the gym, and if I got out of his hold, then one of the other coaches would come and help him get me back down—two coaches against one high school kid. They used to frustrate me to the point where it made me cry—and then they'd laugh and call me 'crybaby.'

"Coach Pulliam stayed on me for the rest of my sophomore year and into my junior year. One day, us kids were playing basketball against some coaches in the gym. Coach Pulliam kept fouling me, and I just kept putting up with it. I made this move to the basket, and Coach Pulliam elbowed me hard in the chest. He did it on purpose, and it really hurt. I slammed the basketball down and walked off the court. I was mad and I was crying. Some of my friends said, 'Don't let him get to you!' I just said, 'I'm tired of him doing me this way,' and I went to the locker room and sat on a bench and cried.

"A little later, Coach Pulliam came into the locker room, and I thought, 'Finally, he's coming to say he's sorry.' Years later, I found out that some of the other coaches told him he ought to apologize. But he didn't. He grabbed the front of my shirt and said, 'If you think I'm gonna apologize, you might as well go back out and get ready for your next whupping. I'm gonna keep kicking your butt until you fight me back.' So I took up his challenge and I fought him back."

Talk about the *IMPACT* of a leader's influence! From then on, when Coach Pulliam elbowed Reggie, Reggie threw an elbow back. When they wrestled, Reggie fought and fought until he won. The first time he beat Coach Pulliam on the wrestling mat, the defeated coach asked Reggie to give him a rematch. Reggie replied, "I don't gotta give you nothing! I've got the championship now." Coach insisted, so Reggie wrestled him a second time—and beat him again in front of all of Reggie's teammates.

"I took a lot of pride in beating him," Reggie recalled. "Years later, I called Coach Pulliam. I said, 'I figured out why you were so hard on me back then, and I want to thank you. I used to think you were gonna kill me, but I know you were making me tough. You did a good job.'

"Coach Pulliam said, 'It's funny you would say that, because when you were in high school, I called the parents of all you guys and asked if I could be hard on you in order to build your confidence. Your mother was the only one who said yes.' That blew me away. All that time, I never knew my mother was in on what Coach Pulliam was doing. She let Coach put me through all that. When Coach Pulliam told me that, I was like, 'Thank God for my mother, man!' Because I wouldn't have made it in the NFL any other way."

After high school, Reggie went on to the University of Tennessee—Coach Pulliam's alma mater—where he played for the legendary coach Johnny Majors. After college and a stint in the ill-fated United States Football League, Reggie signed with the Philadelphia Eagles. There he played for Buddy Ryan, the notoriously hard-nosed former defensive coordinator for the Chicago Bears. When Reggie arrived for his first mini-camp under Coach Ryan, he was nervous. He wondered if he could get along with his new coach.

"The first day," Reggie recalled, "Buddy came to me and asked, 'How's your wife?' Sara was pregnant with our first child, Jeremy. I said, 'She's doing good.' 'When's the baby coming?' I said, 'In May.' He said, 'Make sure you spend plenty of time with your wife. Family's the most important thing. This is a great game, but family's number one.' I was glad to hear him say that. I knew the man really cared."

Eagles training camp was a nightmare for Reggie and his teammates. August heat and high humidity combined with intense workouts caused many players to drop from dehydration, heat prostration, and sheer frustration. Reggie saw a number of highly paid teammates throw down their helmets and quit the team under Buddy Ryan's relentless training regimen. For Reggie, there was one sweet oasis in that desert of suffering.

"Buddy came up to me," he recalled, "and he said something that shocked me. He said, 'Reggie, I want you to know that you're the best defensive lineman I've ever seen. You do some things I haven't seen guys do before.' That was a high compliment. To this day, I don't know if Buddy was trying to motivate me or humble me, but I took it as a challenge to be worthy of his praise. I worked harder for Buddy Ryan than any other coach I had ever played for up to that time. That year, I had eighteen sacks. I respect tough coaches, and Buddy is one of the toughest. He was demanding but fair."

The moral of these stories about Reggie White and his coaches is that leaders can be hard-nosed, competitive, and intensely committed to winning—yet equally committed to influencing and caring for their players or subordinates. Toughness and influence are not mutually exclusive. In fact, toughness is often the influence a subordinate needs in order to achieve his or her full potential.

Leadership is not about being the boss. It's about being a servant who cares about influencing others. Leaders of influence care about the good of individuals, not just the success of the organization.

How to Lead through Influence

Let me suggest some practical ways to become a more effective leader of influence. These are insights you can instantly put into practice in any leadership arena, from the ball field to the battlefield, from the boardroom to the classroom.

1. *As the leader, you set an example of confidence, optimism, courage, perseverance, and hard work.* Your subordinates look to you for inspiration and reassurance. If you appear tentative or pessimistic, they'll become anxious and alarmed. If they see you slacking off, they will become lazy. But if they see that you are fired up and ready to conquer the world, their morale and motivation will soar.

Dr. William A. Cohen is a retired major general (U.S. Air Force Reserve) who also lived and served in Israel and flew missions during the Yom Kippur War, October 1973. He is also president of the Institute of Leader Arts. He tells the story of the ancient Greek soldier-philosopher Xenophon, who accompanied a Greek mercenary force that invaded Persia. At one point, Xenophon addressed the captains of the army and gave them these instructions on leadership:

1. Leaders set the example. If you are downhearted, your men will become cowards. If you are clearly prepared to meet the enemy and call on your soldiers to do their part, you can be sure they will try to emulate you.
2. Leaders need to be braver than those they lead, and must be the first to do hard work.
3. Leaders must be in control and exercise discipline, otherwise nothing useful ever gets done.
4. Leaders train their soldiers to think about positive action that each must take to be successful, otherwise they think about "What is going to happen to me?"[9]

Cohen also describes how Xenophon set an example for his troops. Xenophon rode on horseback at the head of a column of infantry, clad in the heavy armor of the cavalry. When he heard one of the foot soldiers behind him complaining that he had to walk, burdened by a heavy shield, while the commander rode on horseback, Xenophon leaped from his horse, took the shield from the complaining soldier's hands, and shoved him out of the ranks.

Then Xenophon continued to lead the column—but on foot, not on horseback. Though he still wore the heavy armor of the cavalry, he also carried the infantryman's shield. Though he bore twice the burden of his men, Xenophon set the pace and encouraged the troops to keep up with him.[10]

Author and futurist Ian Morrison says that a leader must be the CEO of the organization—the "Chief Example Officer." Subordinates, he says, "want to be motivated, inspired, and moved to action. . . . They will perform if they believe. But what makes them believers? More and more, employees pay attention to the leader's behavior. . . . In the best organizations, leaders inspire followers by their actions and behavior much more than by their speeches."[11]

2. *Set an example of integrity in even the smallest things.* Our influence requires that we maintain congruence between our walk and our talk. No one is perfect, but we have to strive to live a life that honestly, consistently reflects our values. Our children, colleagues, and subordinates are watching us and taking their cue from us. They know if we are cutting legal and ethical corners, even in minor matters—and they will pattern their own character and actions after ours.

Back in the days before email, a son wrote a letter to his dad which began, "Hey, Dad, this letter is free. The post office didn't cancel the stamp on your last letter to me, so I reused it." The following week, he received a letter from his dad. Unfolding the letter, the young man found that his father had pasted a new stamp at the top of the letter, then had drawn a big, black X through the stamp. Below that, his father had written, "Dear son, your debt to the United States government has been paid. Love, Dad."

That's an important lesson for all of us as leaders to teach—fathers to children, executives to employees, professors to students, pastors to parishioners, commanders to troops: Maintain your integrity in the small things and the big things will take care of themselves. As Tony Simons writes in *The Integrity Dividend*, "Your subordinates will tend to emulate the level of integrity you display, and that shapes how they will approach their subordinates and how they will approach you."[12]

In *The Power of Ethical Management*, Ken Blanchard and Norman Vincent Peale suggest a template for ethical decision making—a three-question quiz they call The Ethics Check. Question 1: "Is it legal?" Will this decision accord with the laws of society, the policies of my organization, and my personal principles and values? Question 2: "Is it balanced?" Will this decision create a winner and a loser—or will it be balanced and fair toward everyone concerned? Question 3: "How will it make me feel about myself?" If my decision were exposed to public inspection, would I be proud of it—or would I feel ashamed? What if my family knew? If we would filter every leadership decision through this simple three-question test, we would safeguard our personal ethics, our leadership reputation, and our influence.

3. Influence people—don't "manage" them. Midwestern retail entrepreneur Frederik G. H. Meijer was a leader in the realm of one-stop-shopping discount stores. When he died at age ninety-one in December 2011 in Grand Rapids, Michigan, the Meijer Corporation was the fifteenth-largest privately held company (by revenue), with two hundred stores in five states. Meijer once expressed his leadership philosophy this way: "You manage change, problems, and emergencies. But you never manage people. You help them improve and, if needed, you become their mentor."

Meijer's approach not only contributed to his retail success, but won him many admirers among his employees. His *New York Times* obituary observed:

> On a memorial Web site, several employees wrote about the personal interest Mr. Meijer took in them. He would speak to Frank Wesolowski in Polish, encouraging him to learn a few words of Polish to make his grandmother proud. Dorothy DeRuiter-Berkenpas, who worked at a store in Grand Rapids, remembered that when she needed a special phone that was compatible with her hearing aids, Mr. Meijer came in to make sure she had received the right equipment.[13]

Clearly, Frederik Meijer was much more than a "boss." He was a leader of influence, and his employees were deeply and positively impacted by the way he cared for them.

When the Philadelphia 76ers traded Wilt Chamberlain to the Los Angeles Lakers in 1968, Coach John Wooden attended the Wilt Chamberlain press conference in L.A. A sportswriter asked Chamberlain: "Do you think that [Lakers coach] Bill van Breda Kolff can handle you?"

"No one handles me," Chamberlain replied. "I am a person, not a thing. You handle things. You work with people. I think I can work with anyone."

Chamberlain's answer profoundly impacted Coach Wooden's thinking. This press conference occurred shortly after Coach Wooden's book *Practical Modern Basketball* had been published. "I had a section in this book entitled, 'Handling Your Players,'" Coach recalled. "I left this meeting, came home and took my book and . . . crossed out, 'handling your players,' put 'working with your players.' And any place that I had alluded to handling your players, I changed. I called the publisher and wanted that correction made for any future editions."[14]

4. *Use indirection as an influence and leadership tool.* Do you want to raise morale? Do you want to boost the loyalty or confidence level of your subordinates? Would you like to congratulate and empower your subordinates in a powerful way? Then consider the power of indirection.

Indirection is a process of influencing people by conveying a message to them through roundabout channels instead of direct communication. One of the best examples of indirection comes from Michael Abrashoff, who at age thirty-six became one of the youngest commanding officers in the Pacific Fleet when he took charge of the USS *Benfold*. Under his command, the *Benfold* was transformed from one of the most dispirited and inefficient ships in the fleet to one of the finest, most combat-ready ships. Now retired from the navy, Abrashoff is a leadership speaker and author.

Soon after becoming captain of the *Benfold*, Michael Abrashoff realized he had a severe morale problem on board. His plan for raising morale: Indirection. Instead of praising his sailors directly, he wrote letters to the parents of his crew, praising their sons whenever they showed character, initiative, or improvement. Once, when he learned that the parents of one crewman were recently divorced, he wrote to both parents. Sometime later, the sailor reported to Captain Abrashoff with tears in his eyes. He could barely speak because of his emotions.

"What's wrong?" Captain Abrashoff asked.

"I just got a call from my father," the sailor replied. "All my life, he told me I'm a failure. This time, he said he'd just read your letter, and he wanted to congratulate me and say how proud he was of me. It's the first time in my entire life he's actually encouraged me. Captain, I can't thank you enough."

Hearing those words, Captain Abrashoff himself was nearly moved to tears.[15]

That was one of many turning points that transformed the morale and performance level of the USS *Benfold*, enabling the crew to win the coveted Spokane Trophy for most combat-ready ship in the fleet. Captain Abrashoff found that he got the best results through indirect means, commending the crew not to their faces, but to their parents.

The next time you want to achieve great things through your leadership influence, consider the indirect approach. You may find that you can accomplish lofty goals and motivate your people in a more powerful way by speaking well of them behind their backs.

5. Don't solve problems for your subordinates. Your job as a leader of influence is to equip your people to solve their own problems. That means you must resist the temptation to solve their problems for them. You can and should influence them by talking it through with them, asking them questions, and helping them explore options—but if possible, let them find their own solutions. Avoid dictating solutions to them.

When I was in my twenties and working as general manager of the Spartanburg Phillies, I was constantly encountering problems I had never faced before. I would take these problems to Mr. Littlejohn and ask him what to do. And he would almost *never* tell me how to solve my problem! In fact, it seemed to *delight* him whenever I had a new problem to solve. He genuinely enjoyed watching me wrestle with a dilemma. No, he didn't take pleasure in my misery. Rather, as a leader of influence, he was interested in my personal and professional growth and maturity.

"Don't run from your problems," he'd always tell me. "Problems give you a wonderful chance to sell yourself to others. Anybody can operate in the good times. But during the tough times, you can really make an impression on people when you prove that you are able to solve problems."

It's annoying when your boss seems so downright cheerful about your problems! But looking back, I see that Mr. Littlejohn knew what he was doing. Solving my own problems was good for me.

I had a similar experience with another leader of influence when I was in Chicago, working with the Chicago Bulls. Over lunch with my pastor, Dr. Warren Wiersbe, I told him about some problems I was dealing with. I looked to him for some answers—or at least some sympathy. Instead, Dr. Wiersbe responded with the same annoying cheeriness I had previously seen in Mr. Littlejohn. "Now, Pat," Dr. Wiersbe said, "don't waste your sufferings. Life is full of problems, so you might as well put them to good use and learn from them."

This principle of leadership wisdom is as old as the Bible. The apostle James instructs us:

> When all kinds of trials and temptations crowd into your lives my brothers, don't resent them as intruders, but welcome them as friends! Realise that they come to test your faith and to produce in you the quality of endurance. But let the process go on until that endurance is fully developed, and you will find you have become men of mature character with the right sort of independence.
>
> James 1:2–4, PHILLIPS

Even at my age, I still have problems to face and lessons to learn. I don't like problems any more today than I did when I was in my twenties. But I know that I've experienced the greatest growth in my life when my leaders and mentors have influenced me by letting me solve my own problems.

6. Be a good listener. Leaders of influence listen to their people. They listen before speaking. They ask open-ended questions that cannot be answered with a simple "yes" or "no." They listen for feelings, not just facts. They are comfortable letting subordinates express emotions and even vent their anger (in a respectful way). They even take time to draw out the opinions and emotions of their subordinates.

The late Chuck Daly was one of the elite coaches in NBA history. Chuck and I worked together with both the Philadelphia 76ers and the Orlando Magic. He once told me about a lesson he learned when he coached Julius Erving and the 76ers. Julius approached Chuck and said, "Do you know where every player on this team likes to shoot from?" The reason he asked was that Chuck, like many coaches, tended to design plays without regard for the players' own preferences. Julius had his own "sweet spot" that he liked to shoot from, and other players had different locations on the court that worked best for them. "Ever since Julius pointed that out to me," Chuck concluded, "I made it a point to learn where every player felt comfortable shooting from—then I would design a play that would get him a shot from that spot on the court."

Baseball manager Sparky Anderson made a similar point in his book *They Call Me Sparky*. He wrote: "If a manager or a teacher or any kind of boss is smart, he's gonna learn as much from the people he's leading as they're gonna learn from him. You learn how people act in certain situations; then, you make adjustments so that next time is always better than the last. If a person can't do one thing maybe he can do something else—but you ain't gonna know if you don't learn from those around you."[16]

Leaders of influence understand that influence is a two-way street. When we listen, we learn. The unwillingness or inability to listen to subordinates is the Achilles heel of many an otherwise-successful leader. Some leaders are unwilling to admit that the people they lead might know something they don't or have skills that they lack. But the most effective and influential leaders *want* to have people who are more knowledgeable in some areas—that's why they hired them. As leaders, we should go out of our way to recruit people who possess skills and knowledge that we lack.

Then we should listen to what they have to say.

7. *Remain humble—never lose the common touch.* Leaders of influence maintain the attitude of a humble servant. They

know that when their ego no longer fits through the doorway, influence goes out the window.

The Economist magazine calls Rick Warren, pastor of California's Saddleback Church, "arguably the most influential evangelical pastor in America." He authored *The Purpose Driven Life*, one of the bestselling books of all time, and says that his mission as a leader is to attack "the five 'Global Goliaths'—spiritual emptiness, egocentric leadership, extreme poverty, pandemic disease, and illiteracy and poor education." Egocentric leadership, of course, is the opposite of influential leadership, because egocentric leadership is about an individual's ambition for power. Influential leadership is about empowering others.

That's why Rick Warren is focused on influence rather than power, humility rather than ambition. In a 2005 interview with *Newsweek*, Warren said:

> I was reading the Bible one day and I came to Psalm 72, Solomon's prayer for more influence.[17] He asked God to make him famous; he said, bless me and give me power. It sounds like the most egotistical prayer until you read his reasons. It was so that as king he could defend the defenseless, speak up for the poor, the disabled, the marginalized. I realized the purpose of influence is to speak up for those who have no influence. That was a turning point.[18]

The late Anglican evangelical churchman John R. W. Stott expressed a similar view in his book *Issues Facing Christians Today*: "The authority by which the Christian leader leads is not power but love, not force but example, not coercion but reasoned persuasion. Leaders have power, but power is safe only in the hands of those who humble themselves to serve."[19] Leaders who are genuinely humble treat everyone as equals because it is simply not in their hearts to see anyone as "inferior."

A few years after the tragic death of Diana, Princess of Wales, I had dinner with an English business leader, Graham Lacey, who was personally acquainted with her. I asked him, "If Princess Diana could be with us right now, what would she do and say?"

"For one thing," Lacey replied, "the princess would be fascinated with all of your nineteen children. She would want to go to your home and meet each one. She'd be completely uninhibited about getting down on the floor and playing with the younger children. And after returning home to England, she would send each of your children a handwritten note, and remember each one at Christmastime with a card."

That description spoke volumes to me of this gracious and influential leader, Princess Diana, who captivated everyone who met her. It was not her "royalty" that dazzled people so much as her common touch—her personal warmth and elegant humility. That is a quality that all of us, as leaders of influence, need to emulate and cultivate.

Living and Dying to Influence Others

Auschwitz, the notorious Nazi death camp in southern Poland, had a cruel and deadly rule: If one prisoner escaped, ten would be chosen to die in his place. In late July 1941, an escaped prisoner caused this brutal rule to be invoked. The prison guard assembled a group of prisoners in the yard and randomly selected ten men to die a horrible, lingering death by starvation in Cell 18, the feared "hunger bunker" of Auschwitz.

One of the ten condemned men, a Polish army sergeant, Francis Gajowniczek, cried out, "My wife, my children! I'll never see them again!" as the SS guards prodded him toward the starvation bunker.

Just then, another prisoner stepped forward and said, "Let me take his place." This prisoner was a Catholic priest, Father Maksymilian Kolbe, Prisoner Number 16670. Arrested in February 1941 for helping to hide Polish Jews, Father Kolbe was deported to Auschwitz in May. He was a self-sacrificing leader of the prisoners who had often gone without food so that others could eat his share. Now he was offering his life in place of the life of Sergeant Gajowniczek. The Kommandant agreed, and Father Kolbe was sent to Cell 18 in place of the Polish sergeant.

Every day for the next two weeks, a worker would go into the starvation bunker to remove the bodies of those who had died. The bodies would then be fed to the crematorium. At other times when prisoners had been condemned to Cell 18, the prisoners would curse the guards. But the group led by Father Kolbe did not curse. When the guards came into the bunker, they found Kolbe and his fellow prisoners praying or singing hymns. Whenever a dying prisoner began to slip into delirium or a coma, Father Kolbe would pray with him and administer last rites. One by one, the prisoners of Cell 18 died and their bodies were removed.

After two weeks of slow starvation, four prisoners still lived, but only one was conscious—Father Kolbe himself. On August 14, the SS guards entered the bunker along with the camp doctor. The doctor administered a lethal injection of carbolic acid to each man. When the doctor came to Father Kolbe, the doomed priest raised his arm to receive the hypodermic needle. He prayed aloud as the doctor injected the solution.

Even the SS guards were amazed as they watched Father Maksymilian Kolbe die. One was so impressed that he wrote a record of Father Kolbe's death, preserving his story for history.[20]

Father Kolbe lived and died as a leader of influence. Until his very last breath, he served others, empowered others, encouraged others, and set an example for others to follow. That's a great way for a leader of influence to live—and an even greater way to die.

Questions for Group Discussion or Individual Reflection

Chapter 8: Be a Leader of Influence

1. Before reading this chapter, did you see yourself as a leader? Does the statement that leadership equals influence change your view of yourself as a leader?

In what arenas of your life do you have a leadership or influence role? In your family? Your workplace? Your church? Your community? Elsewhere? Who are the people you lead and influence? Think of specific, recent examples that describe your leadership and influence style.

2. The author lists seven "sides" or ingredients of leadership: vision, communication skills, people skills, character, competence, boldness, and servanthood. Which of these seven sides of leadership are you strong in? Which are areas of weakness for you?

   Of the leadership strengths you possess, which were natural gifts or talents? Which were acquired skills? In which area or areas of leadership would you like to grow stronger? What are some specific steps you could take this week to improve your leadership skills?

3. What are some specific ways that you can build stronger leadership traits into your children? Into your subordinates or players?

4. The author tells the story of Reggie White and his high school coach, Robert Pulliam. Coach Pulliam was unrelentingly tough on Reggie. Do you agree or disagree with the way Coach Pulliam attempted to influence the young football player? Would this approach work with everybody? Would you ever use a similar approach?

   Years later, Reggie White learned that Coach Pulliam had asked Reggie's mother for permission to go hard on him, and she agreed. If you had been Reggie's mother, would you have agreed to Coach Pulliam's request?

5. The author suggests using "indirection" as a tool of influence and leadership. Has a leader ever used indirection toward you? What was the result?

   Have you ever used indirection in your own leadership role? Did it produce the desired result?

6. When your children or subordinates bring you their problems, do you tend to solve those problems or do you encourage them to keep searching for solutions? Do you agree with the author's advice? How does the author's counsel affect the way you lead and influence others in the future?

9

Be a Christian of Influence

Every life is a profession of faith, and exercises an
inevitable and silent influence.

Philosopher Henri-Frédéric Amiel[1]

*T*he Indiana Pacers were in Orlando for the first exhibition
game of the 1996 season. About ten minutes before the game
was to start, I ran into Roger "The Rajah" Brown. Roger was
a legend in the American Basketball Association, appearing in
four All-Star games and earning three championship rings. At
age fifty-four, Roger still looked trim and athletic.

I hadn't seen Roger in a long time, so I called out to him and
said, "Hey, Roger! How are you doing?"

He smiled and shook my hand. "Pat," he said, "I've got
cancer."

I was stunned. "Roger," I said, "I'm sorry to hear that. Tell
me what happened."

"I started having abdominal pains this past spring," he said,
"so I went in to have it checked out. When they opened me up,
they found that the cancer was in my liver, my intestines, and

185

other places. So they just closed me up and told me I had six months to live."

Roger had been candid with me, so I decided to be just as candid with him. I silently prayed for wisdom and the right words to speak, then I said, "Roger, do you know where you'll go when you die? We all have to die one day, but if you know Jesus Christ, you'll be assured of eternal life with him."

"Yes, I know Jesus," he told me. "And I know I'll be well taken care of when the time comes." He seemed at peace—even optimistic. "Well, Pat, it's great to see you again. It ought to be a good game."

I was sad that Roger Brown's time on earth was so limited, yet I was glad that he had such a strong assurance of eternity with God. Roger Brown passed away in March 1997, about five months after that conversation. But I do believe I'll see him again.

On the Outside Looking In

No one person led me to faith in Christ. I had many spiritual "fathers" and "mothers" who played an influential role in my relationship with God. All of these influences came together in February 1968, when I was the twenty-seven-year-old general manager of the Spartanburg Phillies.

One of those influences was Bobby Malkmus, the former Phillies infielder, who came to Spartanburg to coach our young ballplayers. Though I was excited about Bobby working with our team, he had a reputation as someone who was *very* religious. This was during my pre-Christian years, and to be candid, I was worried about getting buttonholed by a Bible-thumping religious zealot.

Only after I got to know Bobby did I realize that he was actually an easygoing guy with a deep but quiet faith—not a fanatic at all. Before long, I realized that there was something about the confident way he lived his life that made me want to be like him. I began to wonder what Bobby Malkmus had that I was missing.

Around the same time, I brought a strong man named Paul Anderson to our ballpark to do a promotional show. Paul had won a gold medal at the 1956 Olympic Games in Melbourne, Australia, and was once listed in the *Guinness Book of World Records* for a backlift of 6,270 pounds. During our show, he lifted a wooden platform on his back with eight of our beefiest ballplayers sitting on it. The crowd went wild. After these feats of strength, he spoke to the crowd.

"I've lifted more weight than anyone in the history of mankind," he said. "I've been written up in Ripley's *Believe It or Not*. They call me the strongest man in the world. But I want you to know that I, Paul Anderson, the strongest man in the world, can't get through a minute of the day without Jesus Christ. If I can't make it through life without Christ, how about you?"

The crowd hadn't expected to hear a sermon at a baseball game—and neither had I. But the fans gave Paul Anderson one of the biggest ovations I had ever heard. I thought, *Wow, that's something I could never do—get up and talk about religion to a bunch of sports fans!* Then it hit me that Paul Anderson hadn't said a word about *religion*. He had talked about *Jesus Christ* as if he were talking about a friend. That was a new concept for me.

One evening, I went to the Spartanburg gym-auditorium to watch a state women's basketball tournament. On the way in, someone handed me a flyer about a singing group, The New Folk, who were giving a concert that same night in the auditorium upstairs. After the first game, I got up and went upstairs to check out the concert.

The New Folk were eight young men and women who sang in the Peter, Paul, and Mary folk style so popular in the 1960s. After performing a few folk standards, they began singing songs about God. Then they took turns talking about "knowing Jesus Christ"—but what they said made no sense to me. How could I "know" someone who died two thousand years ago?

After the concert, I went up to talk to the petite blonde in the group. I found out her name was Sandy Johnson and I tried to impress her with the fact that I was a big-shot sports executive—but she kept changing the subject to what God was doing in her life. She handed me a booklet to read, and I stuck it in my pocket. I had tried my best to connect with this girl, and she had deflected me with ease. Though I found her attractive, there was something else she had—a radiance, an assurance—that I wanted in my own life. I had seen this same quality in my boss, Mr. Littlejohn, and I had seen it in Bobby Malkmus and Paul Anderson. I had to find out what it was.

Returning home that night, I flopped onto my bed—and I felt that booklet jabbing me from my pocket. I took it out and saw that it was called *Have You Heard of the Four Spiritual Laws?* It only took a couple of minutes to read—but when I finished, it was as if a light came on in my mind.

"Is *that* what makes those people different? Is *that* the 'something' I see in Sandy Johnson and Mr. Littlejohn and Bobby Malkmus and Paul Anderson? Is *that* why, in spite of my success and my money, I'm still unhappy?" I had to know more.

On a hunch, I called the motel nearest the auditorium where The New Folk had performed—and yes, they were staying there. I asked for Sandy Johnson's room. Moments later, I heard her voice: "Hello?"

"Sandy Johnson? This is Pat Williams. I need to talk to you again. Let me buy you breakfast."

"We're leaving town at eleven—"

"Great," I said, "I'll see you at nine-thirty."

She probably thought I was stalking her! But she agreed to have breakfast with me.

I awoke early the next morning. When I heard my roommate, John Gordon, begin to stir, I said, "John, tell me what you make of this. It's called *The Four Spiritual Laws.* 'Law One: God loves you and offers a wonderful plan for your life. Law Two: Man is sinful and separated from God. Therefore, he cannot know and experience God's love and plan for his life. Law Three: Jesus Christ is God's only provision for man's sin. Through Him you can know and experience God's love and plan for your life. Law Four: We must individually receive Jesus Christ as Savior and Lord; then we can know and experience God's love and plan for our lives.'"

"What are you reading from?"

"It's a booklet. A girl named Sandy Johnson gave it to me last night. Listen to this—it's from the Bible: 'Behold, I stand at the door and knock; if anyone hears My voice and opens the door, I will come in to him.'"

John nodded thoughtfully. I didn't know it then, but he had been troubled by the same questions that troubled me.

At nine thirty, I met Sandy at the pancake house next to the motel. She was polite but guarded—and who could blame her? But I pulled out the booklet and asked her question after question about The Four Spiritual Laws. We talked until it was time for her to go. I was still asking questions as she climbed into the van with the other singers. She waved as the van pulled away, leaving me with many questions still unanswered.

More miserable than ever, I went back to work, made a few sales calls, then headed to the ballpark. I couldn't concentrate. Something was all wrong inside me.

Finally, I decided to ask the one man who was *sure* to know what it all meant—Mr. Littlejohn. I jumped into my car and dashed to his office—and was surprised to find John Gordon and a local minister, Rev. Alister Walker, arriving at the same time. We went inside together, and Rev. Walker announced in his Scottish brogue, "I've got some wonderful news! John Gordon has committed his life to Jesus Christ!"

Now, that was a shock. I had no clue that John had agonized for days over his own spiritual condition, just as I had. The words I had read to him from the booklet had been a catalyst for his decision to surrender his life to Christ. So he had sought out Rev. Walker and asked him to explain to him how to become a Christian—and he had made his decision.

So John, Rev. Walker, Mr. Littlejohn, and I sat together in the office, and the three of them talked excitedly about John's decision. I sat there dumbfounded, wishing someone would explain it to me. I felt that John was one of *them* now—a Christian. John had that same look of assurance and joy that Sandy Johnson and the others had—

And I was on the outside looking in.

Finally, John and Rev. Walker left, and I was alone with Mr. Littlejohn. There was a long silence, then Mr. Littlejohn said, "Pat, Rev. Walker and I have been praying for you. My wife and I have been praying for you ever since you came to Spartanburg. You know, if you're ready, you could make the same decision Johnny made today."

I knew it was time. I knew what the Four Spiritual Laws were all about. I knew that God loved me and wanted to make my life meaningful and full. Most of all, I finally understood the decision I had to make. It was time for me to stop living for my own ambitions, my own agenda. It was time to let Jesus Christ set the direction for the rest of my life.

Some people pray a prayer of commitment when they reach that moment of surrender. I didn't need any words. The decision was already made deep within me, and nothing could ever unmake that decision. I had given my life to Jesus Christ. I felt I had been scrubbed clean from the inside out. I'm not ashamed to admit that, at that moment, I began to cry.

Mr. Littlejohn, Bobby Malkmus, Paul Anderson, and Sandy Johnson and The New Folk were just a few of the people who influenced my decision to turn my life over to Jesus Christ. God used many other people to lead me to him. As Paul writes in 1 Corinthians 3, some plant God's message, others water it, but it's God who makes it grow.

At times, you may be the one who plants a seed of the good news of Jesus Christ. At other times, you may be the one who waters. But if you make yourself available to the One who makes it grow, you'll be a Christian of influence—someone God uses to change lives and draw people to himself.

Let me suggest several specific actions you can take on a daily basis to become a Christian of influence:

Prayer Is Influence

Many people treat prayer as a last resort: "Well, I guess there's nothing left to do but pray." But Christians who truly understand God's power know that prayer is the most potent instrument of influence we have. If we truly want to influence our world and the people around us, we must begin with prayer.

When the word went out that I had been diagnosed with cancer, I received letters, emails, and calls from people I had never met, assuring me of their prayers. When you go through a life-threatening experience, sustained by the prayers of other people, you truly can feel it. You can tell that something supernatural is taking place in your life, in your circumstances, in your spirit, in your emotion, and yes, in the cells of your body.

Prayer is influence.

There's an Orlando-area pastor named Basil who calls me about once a month. I've never met him. I don't know much about him. But I do know this: Basil prays for me daily. He called me the first time shortly after the news of my cancer went public. When he calls, he says, "Pat, how are you doing? Let me pray with you. God has placed you on my heart." And he'll pray for me right over the phone—and his prayers always touch a real need in my life. He has impacted my life with his influence through prayer, through the power of God.

While this book was being written, a basketball sensation exploded on the scene. Jeremy Lin is a 6' 3" point guard from Harvard who played without a scholarship because his first-choice schools, Stanford and UCLA, turned him down. After graduation, he went unclaimed in the 2010 NBA draft, but later signed with the Golden State Warriors (based in Oakland, not far from Lin's hometown of Palo Alto, California). During Lin's first two years in the NBA, he was waived by the Warriors and the Houston Rockets.

The New York Knicks claimed Jeremy Lin off waivers just after Christmas 2011. He was at the bottom of the Knicks roster, a third-stringer competing for a backup spot. In January 2012, he learned that the Knicks were considering releasing him.

On January 27, the Knicks went to Miami to play the Heat, and Lin attended the pregame chapel. When the pastor asked if there were any prayer requests, Lin raised his hand and said, "Can you pray I don't get cut?"[2] The pastor and the other players prayed for him, then both teams went out and played. Lin sat on the bench throughout the game, and the Knicks lost, 99 to 89.

On February 3, the Knicks played the Boston Celtics. When the Knicks blew a fourth quarter lead and the game was clearly lost, coach Mike D'Antoni gave Lin some playing time. Though Lin couldn't save the game (the Knicks narrowly lost 91–89), he turned in a stunning performance that changed D'Antoni's view of Lin as a backbencher.

Coach D'Antoni rewarded Jeremy Lin with major playing time in the next four games against the Nets, Jazz, Wizards, and Lakers—and the Knicks won all four. Against the Lakers, Lin scored an astonishing 38 points with seven assists—and even outscored the Lakers' Kobe Bryant, who had a 34-point night. Lin averaged 27.3 points, 8.3 assists, and 2.0 steals per game.[3]

Lin and the Knicks just kept winning. On Valentine's Day, Lin scored a buzzer-beating three-pointer to defeat the Raptors. Before Coach D'Antoni gave Jeremy Lin playing time, the 8–15 Knicks had lost 11 of their last 15 games. With Lin in the game, the Knicks went on a seven-game winning streak.

Jeremy Lin made the cover of *Time* and *Sports Illustrated*, and the TV ratings of the New York Knicks nearly doubled overnight. Punsters in the sports writing community were quick to label the media hysteria "Linsanity."

Raised in a Christian home, the son of parents who emigrated from Taiwan in the 1970s, Jeremy Lin uses his influence to share his faith in Jesus Christ. After sealing a win over the Raptors with a three-point clutch shot, he told a reporter, "I just thank my Lord and Savior Jesus Christ for that shot. I'm thankful that it went in. Just a blessing. I'm extremely thankful and extremely humbled."[4]

The only person in the country not infected with Linsanity is Jeremy Lin himself. He's an island of faith, character, and Christian influence in a sea of hype and hysteria. How do you explain the miraculous turnabout in this young man's life? How do you explain the astonishing platform God has given him—a platform Jeremy Lin is using to share his faith?

I say the Jeremy Lin story is one of the most dramatic answers to prayer anyone has ever seen. I believe that when a struggling young basketball player put up his hand and said, "Can you pray I don't get cut?" God said, "Watch *this*!"

Representing Christ

A few years ago, Biola University, a Christian university in southern California, built a beautiful new library on campus. As you walk *into* the library, you see a quotation from the Bible inscribed above the doors—the words Jesus spoke in John 8:12: "I am the light of the world." As you walk *out* of the library and back into the world, you see the words of Jesus from Matthew 5:14: "You are the light of the world."

Jesus is the light of the world—but His light shines through our lives. That's why we, as followers of Jesus, are also the light of the world. He influences and illuminates the world through the light and influence of our lives. But this is only true as long as we follow His example and allow Him to live through us. As someone once said, "Live in such a way that those who know you but don't know God will come to know God because they know you."

The tragedy of unChristlikeness is illustrated by the historical account of Red Jacket and Mr. Cram. "Red Jacket" was the English name given to the Native American leader Sagoyewatha, chief of the Wolf clan of the Seneca tribe. The name "Red

Jacket" referred to a coat given to him by the British during the American Revolution.

In 1805, a New England missionary named Mr. Cram came to preach the gospel to the Seneca people. Mr. Cram encountered resistance among the Senecas because they had been cheated so often by the Europeans. So Mr. Cram went to Red Jacket and asked his help in convincing the Seneca people to receive the Christian gospel. Here's a portion of Red Jacket's reply to Mr. Cram:

> Your forefathers crossed the great water and landed on this island. Their numbers were small. They found friends and not enemies. They told us they had fled from their own country for fear of wicked men and had come here to enjoy their religion. . . . We took pity on them, granted their request, and they sat down among us. We gave them corn and meat; they gave us poison in return. . . .
>
> You have now become a great people, and we have scarcely a place left to spread our blankets. You have got our country, but are not satisfied; you want to force your religion upon us. . . . You say that you are right and we are lost. How do we know this to be true? . . .
>
> Brother, you say you have not come to get our land or our money, but to enlighten our minds. I will now tell you that I have been at your meetings and saw you collect money from the meeting. I can not tell what this money was intended for, but suppose that it was for your minister; and, if we should conform to your way of thinking, perhaps you may want some from us.
>
> Brother, we are told that you have been preaching to the white people in this place. These people are our neighbors. We are acquainted with them. We will wait a little while and see what effect your preaching has upon them. If we find it does them good, makes them honest, and less disposed to cheat Indians, we will then consider again of what you have said.[5]

Red Jacket's words challenge you and me. How do you and I represent Jesus Christ, our example and role model? Has our faith made us more and more like Jesus himself? If not, what reason does anyone around us have to listen to our message or accept our influence?

To be a Christian of influence, pattern your life and your character after your perfect role model, Jesus himself.

Mixing Business and Faith

My longtime friend Otis Smith recently called and asked if he could come for a chat. As a player, Otis was on the roster of the Magic's inaugural season in 1989, and was general manager of the Magic from 2005 to 2012. He came to my house and we talked. He felt a lot of pressure in a stressful job—the same job I had held with teams in Spartanburg, Chicago, Atlanta, Philadelphia, and Orlando. After talking about the demands of the job, Otis asked, "How did you do this for over twenty-five years?"

I told him about my conversion experience as a twenty-seven-year-old baseball executive, and I said, "From that point on, I viewed my life in professional sports as a ministry, not just a career. Yes, it's important to have teams that do well, and fortunately most of the teams I was involved with did well. It's been a successful run. But after I came to Christ, I always viewed my life in sports as a ministry, not just a career.

"We live in a sports-crazy nation, and the influence of an athlete, coach, or sports executive is off the charts in this culture. So I always viewed my job as something far more important than wins and losses, attendance records, and awards. My career is a platform from which to share my values and my faith. That's why I didn't feel the pressure the same way many others do—and I think that's why I was able to continue as long as I did."

Whatever your vocation, you are on the front lines of Christian ministry. Let me give you a couple of examples.

Joseph Vijayam founded Olive Technology in 1996, creating Java applications for the Internet. Today, Olive Technology develops apps for iPhones and Google, designs websites and software products, and produces business solutions. Born in Hyderabad, India, Joseph is a Christian business leader with degrees from Biola University and Georgia State University. He uses his Internet technology skills to encourage Christian influence in the business world. In his blog, Joseph writes:

> Every one of us who is involved in ministry today work from the platforms available to us. Some utilize business, others medicine, and still others education. Platforms are powerful connection points but they must be used wisely and for the right reasons. . . . Look at the platforms that God has you on right now. What platforms will those lead to—are you ready to take full advantage of those next steps?[6]

In an interview for MinistryPlatforms.com, PacMoore founder William Moore said that one of the challenges he faced was a growing—and false—perception that business and faith should never mix. He seeks to build an environment where people think of the workplace as "a place where Jesus and the Bible are viewed as normal." He laments the fact that many Americans have been brainwashed to believe that the Christian faith has no place in the workplace. His goal as CEO of PacMoore is to use his business as a means of influencing his employees, and equipping them to spread God's love to the greater community. He said:

> Our focus is to love our people. . . . Everyone needs to be loved and everyone responds when they see the many ways we try to express our love. One of the key ways we have done it this year is to create a profit sharing program where we pay over 15 percent of profits to our people every month. Love also has a multiplying effect that compounds as people catch the vision and the desire to love all those in their daily work life. I have had countless employees come tell me stories of how PacMoore people have reached out to them. The human soul has a limitless capacity for love when it is filled with the Holy Spirit. People

are transformed when that loves passes through them into the souls of those around them.[7]

So I challenge you: What is your career—and how can you begin using your career as a calling and a ministry to serve and love others in the name of Jesus Christ?

Christlike Grace Under Pressure

Everyone in this world is hurting in some way. If you want to be a Christian of influence, don't pretend that your life is a slide on ice. Be honest about your struggles, your temptations, your times of discouragement. Then explain how your relationship with Christ gets you through those trials.

Andrew Klavan is a novelist and screenwriter. In an article in the *Wall Street Journal*, Klavan said he converted to Christianity in 2004 after thirty-five years of "atheism, agnosticism, deism, [and] Zen."[8] In a 2012 article in the *Journal*, Klavan talked about a baseball player who influenced him in his spiritual journey, Hall of Fame catcher Gary "Kid" Carter.

Gary Carter played most of his twenty-one-year career with the Montreal Expos and the New York Mets. A devout Christian, Carter died at age fifty-seven in February 2012 after a courageous battle with brain cancer. In his tribute to Carter, Klavan recalled that Carter's approach to the game of baseball had impacted him in the 1980s. At that time, Klavan was going through suicidal depression and battling personal demons. Chain-smoking alone in a dark room, Klavan listened to a Mets game on the radio. He recalls:

> Before I knew it, the game had ended and Carter—who apparently had beaten out a grounder to reach first base—was giving a postgame interview. The interviewer asked him how he managed to outrun the throw when his knees were so bad from years of playing catcher. . . .
> I was not a Christian then—not yet—and if Carter had preached religion at that moment, it would have gone right past

me. But he didn't. He said something else, something much simpler but also true . . . . "Sometimes you just have to play in pain."

Carter's words somehow broke through my self-pitying despair. "Play in pain?" I thought. . . . "I can do that. That's one thing I actually know how to do."[9]

Klavan had been looking for solutions to his depression. Gary Carter taught him that when there are no solutions, you simply have to tough it out. And Klavan did tough it out—and eventually found hope in Christ.

Sometimes to be a Christian of influence doesn't mean we have to preach the gospel or share the Four Spiritual Laws. Sometimes it simply means we are honest about our struggles and we tough it out. By doing so, we may give someone else the courage to tough it out as well—and that courage will carry that person through until the light of Jesus shines through the darkness.

I have enjoyed watching the phenomenal career of quarterback Tim Tebow. When he played at the University of Florida, he was the first sophomore to win the Heisman Trophy. He became famous for wearing Bible verses in white lettering on his eye black as a testament to his faith. During the 2009 BCS Championship Game, he sported "John 3:16" on his face. That verse became the highest-ranked search term on Google for the next twenty-four hours—an amazing 94 million hits.[10]

Chosen by the Denver Broncos in the 2010 NFL draft, Tebow was promoted to starting quarterback with the sixth game of the 2011 season. He led the Broncos from a faltering 1–4 start to an 8-8 finish and a wildcard game against the Steelers. In the January 8 playoff game, Tebow completed 10 of 21 passes for a career-topping 316 yards and two touchdowns. The Broncos won in overtime, 29–23.

After the game, reporters noted a string of coincidences in that game: Tebow's passing yards (316), his yards per completion (31.6), and the peak Nielson rating for the game (31.6) all seemed to suggest Tebow's favorite verse, John 3:16. The next day, the top search term on Google was once again "John 3:16."[11]

Though the Broncos were knocked out of the playoffs the following Sunday by the New England Patriots, Tebow continued using his platform to influence others. After the loss, Tebow told reporters, "What I pray before games, during games, after games, is regardless whether I win, whether I lose, whether I'm the hero or the goat, that it doesn't matter, that I still honor the Lord because He's deserving of it. . . . You can be disappointed, but you can still honor the Lord with how you handle things."[12]

Tebow has withstood a great deal of criticism and mockery for his vocal pro-life stance. "There have been a lot of people," he said, "that have been encouraged not to have an abortion because they heard the story of my mom." While Tim's mother Pam was pregnant with him, she contracted amoebic dysentery and went into a coma. To fight the infection, doctors gave her drugs that caused the placenta to detach, depriving the unborn child of oxygen. Believing the baby to be hopelessly impaired, the doctors recommended a therapeutic abortion. Pam prayed for healing instead—and delivered a healthy future Heismann winner.[13]

The backlash against Tim Tebow as a moral and spiritual role model is hard to understand. Ten or twenty years ago, a young man of Tim Tebow's moral fiber and Christian convictions would be treated as a hero. But our culture has become so morally and spiritually corrosive that Tebow has been attacked almost as regularly as he's been praised.

The popular sports blog site BleacherReport.com called Tebow "the most polarizing figure in all of sports."[14] Nonsense. Tim Tebow isn't polarizing at all. He represents the core Judeo-Christian values that our Western culture was founded on—values that have been eroded in recent years. The problem is not a "polarizing" football star, but an already polarized culture. The emergence of Tim Tebow has simply shaken the cultural fault line that already divided our society. It's a division between right and wrong, morality and immorality, godliness and godlessness.

But Tebow always demonstrates grace under pressure—whether on the football field or under fire in the media. As he explained to ESPN interviewer Hannah Storm, "I never listen to outside distractions. That's something I learned very early on at Florida. You're always going to have people talking, you're always going to have naysayers and critics and haters. . . . I can't let that affect me."[15]

You are never too old or too young to take a stand for Christ against the pressure of this unbelieving world. In 2012, I learned about a young lady, just six years old, who demonstrated grace under fire and a strong Christian influence when she was pressured to surrender her faith in Jesus—

And the pressure, I'm sad to say, came from her own father.

Though this six-year-old girl attends a Christian school, her father is an unbeliever. It was Halloween, and the girl's father had a bag in his hands. "Daddy, what's in there?" she asked.

"It's candy," he said.

"Can I have it?"

"Well," her father said, "if you stop believing in Jesus, you can have it."

"Daddy," the child said, "I could never do that."

That's grace under pressure—and that's Christian influence. I pray for this little girl that she will continue to stand strong for Christ throughout her life, and that she will influence her father to believe in Jesus too.

Listen for God's Voice—Then Obey It

Late one night in September 1986, Florida State Seminoles offensive tackle Pablo Lopez got involved in an argument outside a fraternity dance in Tallahassee. Someone grabbed a shotgun and shot Lopez in the abdomen, killing him.

The death of Pablo Lopez was devastating to the entire FSU community. It was especially troubling to Seminoles head coach Bobby Bowden. He called a team meeting the next day—and the subject of the meeting was eternity. He said, "I don't preach to you guys very often, but I'm going to preach to you today. . . . I'm going to talk to you about something that doesn't have anything to do with football, and I want you to listen."

Coach Bowden proceeded to tell his players about faith in Jesus Christ as the way to eternal life. He explained how he himself made a decision to follow Jesus, then added, "All you guys are eighteen to twenty-two and you think you're going to live forever, and Pablo thought the same thing." He pointed to an empty chair and said, "Where is he today? Where are you going to be?"

He concluded his talk by saying, "If any of you want to talk to me about this, my door is always open."

Does a coach at a university have the right to talk about his faith to his players? Coach Bowden will tell you he had not only the right but an urgent calling to level with them about eternity. If any players don't want to be present, they're free to leave.

"But," he adds, "I feel I have a responsibility. These other professors can get you in their classroom and they can talk about communism—that they are communists or atheists—and nobody bothers them. I feel like as a football coach I have a right to tell you what I think is right. . . . I want you all to go to heaven; that's why I express this. It's your choice. I don't want to die without at least telling you what I know."[16]

One of the people in that room was one of Coach Bowden's assistant coaches, Mark Richt, who later recalled:

I stood in the back of the room as Coach Bowden addressed the team about what had happened with Pablo. . . . He was talking to the players, and I just happened to be in the room, but he was speaking to me. All the memories came back to me from the time I had spent during my junior year in college, when I had a roommate, John Peasley, who had presented the Gospel of Jesus Christ to me. . . . While I listened to Coach, all the memories came back from the time I spent with John Peasley, and I became very convinced at that moment that then was the time for me to live for Christ.[17]

Near the end of the meeting, Bobby Bowden told his players, "If any of you here want to talk to me about anything like this, my door is always open."

A short time later, Mark Richt went to Coach Bowden's office and said, "Coach, I know you were speaking to the players, but I hope you don't mind if a young coach comes in and talks to you about it."

Bowden said, "Sure, buddy." And Coach Bowden led Mark Richt to the Lord.[18]

Not long after his conversion to Christ, Mark Richt was named head football coach at the University of Georgia, where he has served for a long time. Today, Mark Richt is one of the most bold and outgoing Christian leaders in college sports today. Thanks to the influence and Christian witness of Bobby Bowden, Mark is absolutely fearless in sharing the good news of Jesus Christ with others.

Don't let yourself be silenced. Listen to that urging within you, telling you to speak up, to bear witness to the hope and faith within you. If faith in Christ were the cure for cancer, would you remain silent? Would you keep it to yourself while people suffered and died from that disease? Of course not. Faith in Christ is the cure for a sickness far worse than cancer—the sickness of sin and eternal death. Don't be silent. Speak up! Take advantage of every opportunity to share your faith.

Don Shinnick was a linebacker for the Baltimore Colts in the Johnny Unitas era, 1957 to 1969. His record of 37 career interceptions still stands today. He played in Super Bowl III, the Colts versus the Jets, January 12, 1969 in Miami. I once talked to Don about his life and career, and he told me the most important decision of his life was when he committed his life to Jesus Christ while at UCLA, thanks to the influence of Bill Bright and Campus Crusade for Christ.

I asked Don what it was like to play in Super Bowl III. "We went into that game as 18-point favorites," he said, "but we ran into a buzz saw. Our quarterback, Johnny Unitas, had a bad elbow, so Coach Shula started Earl Morrall—and Earl threw three interceptions in the first half." In the second quarter, Don almost intercepted a Joe Namath pass intended for wide receiver George Sauer Jr. but had to settle for merely breaking up the play. "I was off-balance and back on my heels," Don said, "but I should've caught it."

When Super Bowl III was over, the Jets had won, 16 to 7—a stunning upset. "Joe Namath had predicted the Jets would win it," Don recalled. "He was right. I was concerned about Joe, about all the cheering and hoopla going to his head. A guy can get a pretty big ego in the NFL. So I went to him out on the field to shake his hand. It was so loud you couldn't hear yourself think. Joe still had his helmet on, and I leaned up close to his ear and shouted, 'Don't forget the Lord, Joe! Don't forget the Lord!'"

Don told me that story a long time ago, but I'll never forget the image of Don Shinnick—this big, tough linebacker who had just spent that past three hours trying to pound Joe Namath into the turf—now reaching out to "Broadway Joe" and reminding him about Jesus. Don Shinnick was committed to using every opportunity to influence others for the Lord Jesus.

Another man who shares that commitment is Wintley Phipps. God has given him the gift of golden baritone pipes. If you've ever heard him sing, you have heard an echo of heaven. He has performed before every president from Jimmy Carter to Barack Obama. Back in October 2000, I heard Wintley Phipps tell a story that was absolutely unforgettable.

In November 1981, Phipps boarded an airliner. As he went to his seat, he noticed a young woman near the front of the plane—a world-famous actress. Taking his seat, Phipps sensed God's voice urging him, "Tell her about me." How should he tell her? Again, he sensed God's voice saying, "Use the talent I gave you."

So Wintley Phipps pulled out a cassette of one of his songs, got out of his seat, and went forward to where the actress was seated. "Excuse me," he said, "I'd like to give you a tape of a song I recorded. It's called, 'Lord, I Give You My Life.'"

The actress accepted the tape and showed him her small cassette player and earphones. "Thank you," she said. "Now I'll have something to listen to on the flight."

Phipps went back to his seat and prayed that God would use his song to speak to the woman's heart. The plane took off and the flight was long and uneventful.

After the plane landed, Phipps walked off the plane—and was surprised to see the actress standing at the gate, waiting for him. As he approached her, she took his hand and said, "Thank you—and God bless you!" Then she hurried away.

Just a few days later, Wintley Phipps saw a photo of the actress on the front page of his morning newspaper. The accompanying story said that the actress, Natalie Wood, had died by drowning during a boat trip near Santa Catalina Island, off the California coast. Only God knows how Natalie Wood's heart and soul were affected by that song of consecration to God—but Wintley Phipps is glad he listened to God's voice and gave Natalie Wood the gift of his music, just before she passed into eternity.

When God speaks to you, seize the moment. Obey His voice. Take advantage of the opportunity. Be a Christian of influence.

Leave a Legacy of Influence

My life was impacted in a huge way by that little booklet published by Campus Crusade for Christ, *Have You Heard of the Four Spiritual Laws?* It was conceived and written by Dr. Bill Bright and his Campus Crusade team. Some years after I came to know Christ in a personal way, I had the privilege of getting to know Bill Bright as a friend, and I told him how that little booklet helped change the course of my life.

For years, Bill suffered from pulmonary fibrosis, a chronic and progressive lung disease. As a result, he often had difficulty breathing. I once visited him at Florida Hospital in Orlando. I found him outside the hospital, sitting in a wheelchair as his wife,

Vonette, pushed him along. The date is etched in my mind—September 10, 2001, the day before the 9/11 terror attacks. I greeted Bill and said, "How are you doing?"

He smiled behind his oxygen mask. "Praising the Lord," he said. That was Bill's attitude, no matter what life threw at him. He was always praising the Lord.

A few months before his death, Bill received a phone call from President George W. Bush. The two men chatted for a few minutes, then Bill began to tire and needed to end the call. "I'm honored, Mr. President," Bill said, "to receive a call from the most powerful man in the world—but soon I'm going to meet Someone far greater."

On July 19, 2003, he went to meet that greater Someone, his Lord Jesus Christ.

After Bill passed away, I visited with Vonette, and she related a conversation she had with Bill as he neared the end of his life. "Why," she had asked him, "does God allow you to go through such suffering?"

"My suffering is very minor," Bill replied. "I'm surrounded by people who love me. Suffering is a matter of perspective. It's not pleasant, but God allows only so much. I'm really so blessed."

That's the perspective of a Christian of influence. I don't doubt that Bill Bright felt his share of fear in facing death—but Bill focused on his blessings, not his sufferings. He focused on his influence, not his infirmities. That's why he had such a great impact on so many lives.

The influence of Bill Bright was a big factor in my conversion to Jesus Christ. There are literally millions of Christians around the world who can make that same claim. What an example of influence Bill has set for us, and what a legacy of influence he has left us.

That's the way I want to live and die—setting an example and leaving a legacy of influence for the Kingdom of God. It's a legacy that will never fade away.

You are the light of the world. Be a Christian of influence.

Questions for Group Discussion or Individual Reflection

Chapter 9: Be a Christian of Influence

1. The author talked about his various spiritual "fathers" and "mothers" who played influential roles in bringing him to a relationship with Jesus Christ. Who are some of the people in your life who brought you to faith? Describe how people have influenced you and the impact they have had on your spiritual life.

2. Do you agree with the statement that God shapes the world through prayer? Do you honestly see prayer as a powerful instrument of influence—or as a last resort in a crisis? Explain your answer.

   Tell about a time when prayer made a major difference in your life.

3. Jesus said, "I am the light of the world," and He said, "You are the light of the world." Do these two statements contradict each other? Do you see yourself as "the light of the world"? Why or why not?

4. What changes do you need to make in your life so that you will be more like Christ?

5. Do you think it is right to mix business with faith? What steps can you take this week to better integrate your faith into your business life? Are you willing to lose money, lose customers, or lose your job in order to have a stronger Christian influence through your career?

6. What do the people around you learn about the Christian faith when they see you experiencing pressure, stress, adversity, or temptation? Would you like to change the way you respond to these problems in your life? What steps can you take right now so that you will be a stronger, more influential Christian in times of adversity?

7. Looking back, do you regret having missed an opportunity to talk to others about your faith in Jesus Christ? Have there been opportunities to influence others for Christ that you are now glad and grateful you took advantage of?

Are you facing a situation right now where you feel God speaking to you and urging you to use your Christian influence? What steps can you take right now to make sure you don't let this opportunity slip away?

Epilogue

Blessed is the influence of one true, loving human soul on another.

English novelist George Eliot (pen name of Mary Anne Evans), 1819–1880[1]

I began writing this book under a death sentence. As I write these closing words, I have just received a reprieve.

In February 2011, I held a press conference and unveiled my T-shirt with the slogan THE MISSION IS REMISSION. One year later, I was able to announce, MISSION ACCOMPLISHED!

But it was a tough battle and multiple myeloma has been a fierce and stubborn opponent. My doctors pumped me with chemo, off and on, for the better part of an entire year. And the chemo, quite frankly, didn't work. It saved me a lot of money on haircuts and razor blades, but (in boxing terms) it failed to deliver a knockout punch to the cancer.

So I told my doctors it was time to empty out their medicine cabinet and throw it all at me. I said (in baseball terms) that I wanted them to give me the "out pitch," their best stuff, the pitch they can rely on to always get the batter out—because I was clearly up against the Babe Ruth of cancers.

So Dr. Yasser Khaled, my myeloma and stem cell transplant specialist, proceeded to harvest healthy stem cells from my blood system—an estimated 4.9 million cells—which they froze and stored. The process of harvesting stem cells isn't painful, but it is long, uncomfortable, and laborious.

They gave me shots to stimulate the stem cells and get them swimming in my bloodstream like fish so they could be caught. Then they plugged me into the machines. I had three lines coming out of my chest—they called it a "tri-fusion"—and my entire blood system flowed through that machine. It filtered out my stem cells and recycled the blood back into my body. I could actually see the stem cell material being collected in a plastic bag.

Once the stem cells were harvested, Dr. Khaled and his assistants gave me a massive chemo blast to kill the remaining cancer cells in my bone marrow.

The doctors tried to explain what they were doing, but it was a Filipino nurse named Nancy who explained it so I could understand. She told me, "It's like a farmer with his field. He plows the soil and prepares it to be a rich treasure of good soil. He's trying to get the soil just right so that it will be good for the seeds, so the crop can grow strong and healthy. The soil is your bone marrow, the seeds are your stem cells, and the crop will be healthy new bone marrow without cancer. Good seed going back into good soil will make you strong and healthy."

Finally, the day came when they thawed out the 4.9 million healthy stem cells and infused them back into my body, where the cells began multiplying and producing healthy new blood cells. The process of transplanting the stem cells required eleven large syringes attached to the outlets on the tri-fusion. The procedure took all day, but there was no pain and I slept through most of it.

The healthy stem cells grafted successfully and began multiplying. Soon after the transplant procedure, the doctors gave me the good news that I was finally in remission.

It was the toughest year of my life, but God was faithful and I have much to be thankful for. What my doctors have accomplished, along with the prayers of so many family members, friends, and people I don't even know, boggles my mind and soul. I wake up every morning in absolute awe and thankfulness for another new day.

I now have three birthdays to celebrate—my physical birthday on May 3, 1940, my spiritual birthday on February 22, 1968, and my remission birthday of February 10, 2012. And I intend to celebrate each one in grand style, surrounded by friends and loved ones.

I know I'm not cured. I'm in remission, but I still have multiple myeloma. My oncologist, Dr. Robert B. Reynolds, told me, "We want to keep you alive as long as we can because there are new technologies coming along all the time. The longer you live, the more benefit you can get from these new discoveries."

Before I underwent the stem cell transplant, I asked Dr. Reynolds, "What's the shortest hospital stay anyone has ever had after a stem cell transplant?"

He said, "Twelve days."

"Doc," I said, "I want to break that record."

"Pat, we're not concerned with breaking any records. Dr. Khaled and I have just one concern, and that's to get you up and fully functioning again so you can continue to influence as many people as you can for as long as possible. That's our only mission."

And that was good for me to hear. When Dr. Reynolds pointed out that the impact of my influence was on the line, he put it in perspective. (But I still kept my stay to ten days and set a new record!)

Now, here's my closing challenge to you: We are all under a death sentence. I am, and so are you. My experience with multiple myeloma has heightened my sense of urgency to live each day to influence others. But none of us knows how long we may have to make our influence felt.

You may have sixty years, or sixty weeks, or just the next sixty minutes. My question to you is: What will you do with the finite amount of time that remains for you? I hope and pray that you will see your life as a mission—a mission to impact as many lives as lastingly and positively as you can.

May the impact of your influence spread far and wide. May your good example of character and faith echo in many lives, and reverberate down through the years.

The difference you make tomorrow begins with the decisions you make today.

Notes

Introduction

1. Andy Stanley, *Visioneering* (Colorado Springs: Multnomah, 1999), 178.

Chapter 1: The Influences That Have Shaped Your Life

1. Mark Tabb, *Living with Less: The Upside of Downsizing Your Life* (Nashville: Broadman & Holman, 2006), 18.

2. Bill Veeck with Ed Linn, *Veeck—As in Wreck: The Autobiography of Bill Veeck* (Chicago: University of Chicago Press, 2001), 117.

3. Tom Peters, "A Handwritten Thank-You Always Welcome," *Chicago Tribune*, February 20, 1995, http://articles.chicagotribune.com/1995-02-20/business/9502200192_1_network-building-for-years-tiniest-personal-touch-pithy-personal-notes.

4. Zig Ziglar, "Being a Difference Maker," GetMotivation.com, http://www.getmotivation.com/motivationblog/2008/04/being-a-difference-maker-by-zig-ziglar/.

5. Rick Warren, *The Purpose Driven Life: What on Earth Am I Here For?* (Grand Rapids: Zondervan, 2002), 297.

6. Anonymous, "Thoughts About Life," MySeniorPortal.com, http://www.myseniorportal.com/cms_contents/show_category_content/Thoughts%20about%20life/583#break.

Chapter 2: Everyone Has Influence

1. Clayton Kershaw with Ellen Kershaw, *Arise: Live Out Your Faith and Dreams on Whatever Field You Find Yourself* (Ventura, CA: Regal, 2011), 139.

2. Larry Platt, "Charles Barkley," Salon.com, May 30, 2000, http://www.salon.com/2000/05/30/barkley/.

3. Charles Barkley, Nike Air commercial, 1993, transcribed by the author from embedded video at http://www.youtube.com/watch?v=nMzdAZ3TjCA.

4. Unsigned editorial, "I'm Not a Role Model," *Newsweek*, June 27, 1993, http://www.thedailybeast.com/newsweek/1993/06/27/i-m-not-a-role-model.html.

5. Ray Robinson, "A Game for Heroes," *Memories and Dreams*, Winter 2011, 40.

6. Sam Grier, "The Street Sweeper—Be the Best at What You Do," SamGrier .com, http://samgrier.com/6/the-street-sweeper-be-the-best-at-what-you-do/.

7. "Hall of Fame Snubs KC's Buck O'Neil," KMBC.com, February 27, 2006, http://www.kmbc.com/r/7509486/detail.html.

8. Arnold Palmer, "Arnold Palmer: A Hard-Charging Interview with the King," *Golf Digest*, January 2000, http://findarticles.com/p/articles/mi_m0HFI/is_1_51/ai_58314352/pg_6/.

9. Jack Nicklaus with Dr. John Tickell, *Golf & Life* (New York: St. Martin's, 2002), 19.

10. Lisa Russell, "Oprah Winfrey," *People*, March 15, 1999, http://www.people .com/people/archive/article/0,,20063616,00.html.

Chapter 3: Healthy Influence: Serving, Mentoring, and Empowerment

1. Ray Bradbury, *Fahrenheit 451* (New York: Simon & Schuster, 1951), 150.

2. Steven Carr Reuben, "The Wisdom of John Wooden," Kehillat Israel Reconstructionist Congregation, July 2010, http://www.kehillatisrael.org/the-wisdom -of-john-wooden.

3. Annie Lowrey, "Big Study Links Good Teachers to Lasting Gain," *New York Times*, January 6, 2012, A1, http://www.nytimes.com/2012/01/06/education/big-study-links-good-teachers-to-lasting-gain.html?_r=3&pagewanted=1&nl=todays headlines&emc=tha23.

4. Center for Education Reform, "U.S. K-12 Facts," *Digest of Education Statistics 2010*, http://www.lwvbellinghamwhatcom.org/files/general_us_k-12_data_qr.pdf.

5. John Salka with Barret Neville, *First In, Last Out: Leadership Lessons from the New York Fire Department* (New York: Penguin, 2005), 203.

6. Paul Bryant with John Underwood, "Part I: I'll Tell You about Football," *Sports Illustrated*, August 15, 1966, http://vault.sportsillustrated.cnn.com/vault/article/magazine/MAG1078879/7/index.htm.

7. David Brinkley, *David Brinkley: 11 Presidents, 4 Wars, 22 Political Conventions, 1 Moon Landing, 3 Assassinations, 2000 Weeks of News and Other Stuff on Television and 18 Years of Growing Up in North Carolina* (New York: Knopf, 1995), 34.

Chapter 4: Character: The Key to Influence

1. Ida Clyde Clarke, "My Suffrage Creed," Western Kentucky University Top-SCHOLAR database, http://digitalcommons.wku.edu/gob6/1/.

2. Brad Winters, "Leadership Quotes by Coach Bear Bryant," CoachLikeAPro .com, http://www.coachlikeapro.com/coach-paul-bear-bryant.html.

3. Associated Press, "Davis Concedes Playoff to Champ Furyk," ESPN Golf, April 19, 2010, http://sports.espn.go.com/golf/news/story?id=5110442.

4. James M. Kouzes and Barry Z. Posner, *The Truth about Leadership: The No-Fads, Heart-of-the-Matter Facts You Need to Know* (San Francisco: Jossey-Bass, 2010), 114–115.

5. Michael Reagan, *The New Reagan Revolution: How Ronald Reagan's Principles Can Restore America's Greatness* (New York: Thomas Dunne: 2011), 306–07.

6. Arthur Ashe with Arnold Rampersad, *Days of Grace: A Memoir* (New York: Ballantine, 1993), 1.

7. Ibid., 4.

8. Elbert Hubbard, *Selected Writings of Elbert Hubbard: Philistia* (New York: William H. Wise, 1922), 20–21.

9. Ernest C. Cowper, letter to Elbert Hubbard II (son of Elbert and Alice Hubbard), March 12, 1916, "Elbert Hubbard," RoycroftCampusCorporation.com, http://www.roycroftcampuscorporation.com/hubbard.html.

Chapter 5: The Influence of Our Actions

1. H. James Birx, *The Encyclopedia of Time: Science, Philosophy, Theology, and Culture*, Vol. 1 (Thousand Oaks, CA: SAGE Publications, 2009), 210.

2. James M. Kouzes, Barry Z. Posner, John C. Maxwell, et al., *Christian Reflections on the Leadership Challenge* (San Francisco: Jossey-Bass, 2006), 12–13.

3. James C. Shaffer, *The Leadership Solution* (New York: McGraw-Hill, 2000), 53.

4. Bob Paeglow, "33 Cents," Dr. Bob's Blog, November 15, 2006, http://drbobcares.org/blog/2006/11/33-cents.html.

5. Bobby Bowden with Steve Ellis, *Bobby Bowden's Tales from the Seminole Sidelines* (Champaign, IL: Sports Publishing LLC, 2004), 165.

6. Bobby Bowden with Steve Bowden, *The Bowden Way: 50 Years of Leadership Wisdom* (Lanham, MD: Taylor Trade Publishing, 2001), 22–23, emphasis in the original.

7. Cal Ripken Jr., "Being a Role Model: Who's Watching You?," Baseball Hall of Fame induction speech, Cooperstown, New York, July 29, 2007, LeadershipNow.com, September 28, 2007, http://www.leadershipnow.com/leadingblog/2007/09/being_a_role_model_whos_watchi.html.

8. Jim Prime and Bill Nowlin, *Ted Williams: The Pursuit of Perfection* (Champaign, IL: Sports Publishing LLC, 2002), 131–132.

9. Lee Iacocca with William Novak, *Iacocca: An Autobiography* (New York: Bantam, 1986), 241–242.

10. William A. Cohen, *Heroic Leadership: Leading with Integrity and Honor* (San Francisco: Jossey-Bass, 2010), ebook, pages unnumbered; Michael Youssef, *15 Secrets to a Wonderful Life: Mastering the Art of Positive Living* (Nashville: Faith Words, 2008), 129.

11. Steve DiMeglio, "Pak-Inspired Park, 19, Grasps Open," *USA Today*, June 30, 2008, http://www.usatoday.com/printedition/sports/20080630/c9lpga30.art.htm.

12. Tony Bennett with Will Friedwald, *The Good Life: The Autobiography of Tony Bennett* (New York: Pocket, 2007), ebook, unnumbered pages.

13. Dennis McCafferty, "Most Caring Athletes," *USA Weekend*, October 12, 2003, http://159.54.226.237/03_issues/031012/031012mcc.html.

14. Michael Wilbon, "McNabb Makes the Boo Birds Fly Away," *Washington Post*, January 24, 2005, page D01, http://www.washingtonpost.com/ac2/wp-dyn/A31437-2005Jan23?language=printer.

15. Peter King, "Open Mouth, Insert Foot," Inside the NFL, SI.com, October 1, 2003, http://sportsillustrated.cnn.com/2003/writers/peter_king/09/30/mcnabb_limbaugh/.

16. Marcus Hayes, "Hopkins Still Thinking about McNabb," Philly.com, May 11, 2011, http://articles.philly.com/2011-05-11/sports/29532616_1_rich-burg-bernard-hopkins-donovan-mcnabb.

17. Wilbon, "McNabb Makes the Boo Birds Fly Away."

Chapter 6: The Influence of Our Words

1. Augustus Woodbury, *Plain Words to Young Men* (Concord, MA: Edson C. Eastman, 1858), 116.

2. Brandon Land, "Professional Athletes as Role Models: Is It Their Job?," BleacherReport.com, April 9, 2010, http://bleacherreport.com/articles/376089-professional-athletes-as-role-models-is-it-their-job.

3. Kim Alexis, *A Model for a Better Future* (Nashville: Thomas Nelson, 1999), 143.

4. Sam Horn, *Take the Bully by the Horns: Stop Unethical, Uncooperative, or Unpleasant People from Running and Ruining Your Life* (New York: St. Martin's Press, 2002), 99.

5. Tom Junod, "Can You Say . . . 'Hero'?," PittsburghInWords.com, 2008, http://www.pittsburghinwords.org/tom_junod.html.

6. Fred Rogers, *The World According to Mister Rogers: Important Things to Remember* (New York, Hyperion, 2003), 150–51.

7. Ana Dutra, "Sprinkles of Pixie Dust," *New York Times*, December 11, 2011, BU9, http://www.nytimes.com/2011/12/11/jobs/ana-dutra-of-korn-ferry-on-helping-people-achieve.html.

8. Bob LaMonte with Robert L. Shook, *Winning the NFL Way: Leadership Lessons from Football's Top Head Coaches* (New York: HarperCollins, 2004), 77–78.

9. James C. Hunter, *The World's Most Powerful Leadership Principle: How to Become a Servant Leader* (New York: Crown, 2004), 47.

10. Coral Davenport, "Betty Ford's Legacy: Wide and Lasting," National Journal.com, July 9, 2011, http://www.nationaljournal.com/whitehouse/betty-ford-s-legacy-wide-and-lasting-20110709.

11. Rosalynn Carter, "Fond Farewells: Betty Ford," *Time*, December 14, 2011, http://www.time.com/time/specials/packages/article/0,28804,2101745_2102136_2102221,00.html.

12. Rebecca Leung, "Morris: 'Reagan Still a Mystery,'" *60 Minutes*, CBSNews.com, December 5, 2007, http://www.cbsnews.com/8301-3475_162-622051.html.

Chapter 7: Be a Parent of Influence

1. John Cumming, *Prophetic Studies: Lectures on the Book of Daniel* (Philadelphia: Lindsay and Blackiston, 1854), 31.

2. James Baldwin, *Nobody Knows My Name: More Notes of a Native Son* (New York: Vintage Books, 1993), 61.

3. Peter Vecsey, "Russell Reflects on Remarkable Career," *Japan Times*, NBA Report, June 27, 2007, http://www.japantimes.co.jp/text/sp20070627pv.html.

4. Dan Kindlon and Michael Thompson, *Raising Cain: Protecting the Emotional Life of Boys* (New York: Ballantine, 2000), 103.

5. Steve Hartman, "Father Read to Daughter Every Night Until College," CBSNews.com, May 9, 2011, http://www.cbsnews.com/video/watch/?id=7365537n; NPR Staff, "Father-Daughter Reading Streak Lasts Nearly 9 Years," NPR Books, June 18, 2011, http://www.npr.org/2011/06/18/137223191/father-daughter-reading-streak-lasts-nearly-9-years.

6. Kindlon and Thompson, 104.

7. *Reach Them to Teach Them*, "Stories of Influence—Coach David Cutcliffe," September 23, 2009, transcribed by the author from embedded video at http://www.youtube.com/watch?v=Bi1iKGOGknQ.

Chapter 8: Be a Leader of Influence

1. Tom Morris, *True Success: A New Philosophy of Excellence* (New York: Berkeley, 1994), 140.

2. John C. Maxwell, *The 21 Most Powerful Minutes in a Leader's Day: Revitalize Your Spirit and Empower Your Leadership* (Nashville: Thomas Nelson, 2000), 17.

3. James C. Hunter, *The World's Most Powerful Leadership Principle: How to Become a Servant Leader* (New York: Crown, 2004), 46.

4. James C. Shaffer, *The Leadership Solution* (New York: McGraw-Hill, 2000), 53–54.

5. Oren Harari, *The Leadership Secrets of Colin Powell* (New York: McGraw-Hill, 2002), 201.

6. Craig Brian Larson, "Idea Files: Great Anecdotes—The Personal Touch," Health CareCommunication.com, August 2, 2007, http://www.healthcarecommunication.com/Main/Articles/Idea_Files_Great_Anecdotes_1399.aspx.

7. Jared Diamond, "The 'Bell Cow' Theory," *Wall Street Journal*, December 21, 2011, http://online.wsj.com/article/SB10001424052970204879004577110731460989536.html.

8. Nathan Aaseng, *African-American Athletes* (New York: Facts On File, 2003), 230.

9. William A. Cohen, *Drucker on Leadership: New Lessons from the Father of Modern Management* (San Francisco: Jossey-Bass, 2010), 124–25.

10. Ibid.

11. Ian Morrison, "Chief Example Officer," *Health Forum Journal*, April/May 2002, http://ianmorrison.com/chief-example-officer/.

12. Tony Simons, *The Integrity Dividend* (San Francisco: Jossey-Bass, 2008), 182.

13. Stephanie Clifford, "Frederik Meijer, 91, Grocery Store Pioneer," *New York Times*, December 7, 2011, http://query.nytimes.com/gst/fullpage.html?res=9901E3DD1639F934A35751C1A9679D8B63.

14. John Wooden interview, "Basketball's Coaching Legend: The Wizard of Westwood," Academy of Achievement, http://www.achievement.org/autodoc/page/woo0int-4.

15. William A. Cohen, *Heroic Leadership: Leading with Integrity and Honor* (San Francisco: Jossey-Bass, 2010), 116–17.

16. Sparky Anderson with Dan Ewald, *They Call Me Sparky* (Ann Arbor, MI: Sleeping Bear Press, 1998), 106.

17. Note: There is some disagreement among Bible scholars as to whether Psalm 72 was written by King Solomon himself or written by King David as a prayer for his son Solomon; either way, Rick Warren's point about the importance of humility and influence in leadership remains valid.

18. Yonah Bookstein, "My Conversation with Pastor Rick," Rabbi Yonah's Blogshul, December 28, 2005, https://rabbiyonah.wordpress.com/2005/12/28/rick-warren/.

19. John R. W. Stott, *Issues Facing Christians Today* (Grand Rapids: Zondervan, 2006), 494.

20. Dan Graves, "Maximilian Kolbe Gave His Life for Another Man," Christianity.com, July 2007, http://www.christianity.com/ChurchHistory/11630770/; Richard Grimm, "Lifesaver Hero: Maximilian Kolbe," MyHero.com, April 28, 2005, http://myhero.com/go/hero.asp?hero=mkolbe; David Binder, "Franciszek Gajowniczek Dead; Priest Died for Him at Auschwitz," *New York Times*, March 15, 1995, http://www.nytimes.com/1995/03/15/obituaries/franciszek-gajowniczek-dead-priest-died-for-him-at-auschwitz.html.

Chapter 9: Be a Christian of Influence

1. Quoted in James Jennings and Karen Casey, *In God's Care: Daily Meditations on Spirituality in Recovery* (Center City, MN: Hazeldon, 1991), August 16 entry.

2. David Hyde: "Heat's Haslem Tells a Story That Puts Lin's Run with Knicks in Context," SunHerald.com, February 22, 2012, http://www.sunherald.com/2012/02/22/3770888/dave-hyde-heats-haslem-tells-a.html.

3. NBA Press Release, "Knicks' Lin, Thunder's Westbrook named Players of the Week," NBA.com, February 13, 2012, http://www.nba.com/2012/news/02/13/players-of-the-week/index.html?ls=iref:nbahpt2.

4. Christine Thomasos, "Jeremy Lin, Tim Tebow Don't Have Much More Than Faith in Common," ChristianPost.com, February 16, 2012, http://global.christianpost.com/news/jeremy-lin-tim-tebow-dont-have-much-more-than-faith-in-common-69600/.

5. Red Jacket (c.1758–1830), "Red Jacket on the Religion of the White Man and the Red," 1805, *The World's Famous Orations: America: I (1761–1837)*, 1906, http://www.bartleby.com/268/8/3.html.

6. Joseph Vijayam, "One Platform Leads to Another," MinistryPlatforms.com, January 24, 2012, http://www.ministryplatforms.com/one-platform-leads-another.

7. Joseph Vijayam, "Impacting Lives Through PacMoore—An Interview with William Moore," MinistryPlatforms.com, November 30, 2011, http://www.ministryplatforms.com/impacting-lives-through-pacmoore-%E2%80%93-interview-william-moore.

8. Andrew Klavan, "Going All the Way," *Wall Street Journal*, December 24, 2004, http://online.wsj.com/article/SB110385111163508971.html.

9. Andrew Klavan, "Gary Carter Showed Me How to Play the Game," *Wall Street Journal*, February 21, 2012, http://online.wsj.com/article/SB100014240529 702048804045772292218268 79122.html?mod=googlenews_wsj.

10. Jeremy Fowler, "Tebow Draws More Attention for Eye-Black Messages," Blogs.OrlandoSentinel.com, September 10, 2009, http://blogs.orlandosentinel.com/sports_college_uf/2009/09/tebow-draws-more-attention-for-eyeblack-messages.html.

11. Glen Levy, "Tim Tebow's 316 Passing Yards Evokes Biblical Number," *Time* NewsFeed, WebCite, January 9, 2012, http://www.webcitation.org/64e9CfA27.

12. Randy Alcorn, Facebook blog post, January 15, 2012, https://www.facebook.com/randyalcorn/posts/10150492428584142.

13. Randy Alcorn, "Doctors Recommended Football Star Tim Tebow Be Aborted," LifeNews.com, January 13, 2012, http://www.lifenews.com/2012/01/13/doctors-recommended-football-star-tim-tebow-be-aborted/.

14. Ken Shepherd, "Bleacher Report: Tim Tebow 'Most Polarizing Figure in All of Sports,'" NewsBusters.org, January 9, 2012, http://newsbusters.org/blogs/ken-shepherd/2012/01/09/bleacherreportcom-tim-tebow-most-polarizing-figure-all-sports.

15. Hannah Storm video, "Face-to-Face—Tim Tebow," ESPN.go.com, February 3, 2012, transcribed by the author from embedded video at http://search.espn.go.com/hannah-storm/videos/6.

16. Bobby Bowden with Steve Ellis, *Bobby Bowden's Tales from the Seminole Sidelines* (Champaign, IL: Sports Publishing LLC, 2004), 163–65.

17. Steve Ellis and Bill Vilona, *Pure Gold: Bobby Bowden—An Inside Look* (Champaign, IL: Sports Publishing LLC, 2006), 135–36.

18. Ibid.

Epilogue

1. Quoted in Erin Gruwell, *The Gigantic Book of Teachers' Wisdom* (New York: Skyhorse, 2007), 26.

Pat Williams is senior vice president of the NBA's Orlando Magic. He has almost fifty years of professional sports experience, has written seventy books, and is one of America's most sought after motivational speakers.

Jim Denney is a writer with more than eighty published books to his credit. His collaborative titles include *Reggie White in the Trenches*, *Undefeated*, *A Model for a Better Future*, and numerous books with Pat Williams, including *Go for the Magic*, and *Coach Wooden*.

CONNECT WITH PAT

We would love to hear from you. Please send your comments about this book to Pat Williams:

pwilliams@orlandomagic.com

Pat Williams
c/o Orlando Magic
8701 Maitland Summit Boulevard
Orlando, FL 32810

If you would like to set up a speaking engagement for Pat, please contact his assistant, Andrew Herdliska:
(407) 916-2401
aherdliska@orlandomagic.com

PatWilliamsMotivate.com

 OrlandoMagicPat

Good Man—
GREAT COACH